PARTICIPATION IN GOD

PARTICIPATION IN GOD

*A Theological Framework for Individual
and Congregational Development*

❧

G. Thomas Luck

WIPF & STOCK · Eugene, Oregon

PARTICIPATION IN GOD
A Theological Framework for Individual and Congregational Development

Copyright © 2024 G. Thomas Luck. All rights reserved. Except for brief quotations in critical publications or reviews, no part of this book may be reproduced in any manner without prior written permission from the publisher. Write: Permissions, Wipf and Stock Publishers, 199 W. 8th Ave., Suite 3, Eugene, OR 97401.

Wipf & Stock
An Imprint of Wipf and Stock Publishers
199 W. 8th Ave., Suite 3
Eugene, OR 97401

www.wipfandstock.com

PAPERBACK ISBN: 978-1-4982-0436-1
HARDCOVER ISBN: 978-1-4982-0438-5
EBOOK ISBN: 978-1-4982-0437-8

Unless otherwise noted, the Scripture quotations contained herein are from the New Revised Standard Version, Updated Edition Bible, copyright © 1989, 2021 by the Division of Christian Education of the National Council of the Churches of Christ in the U.S.A., and are used by permission. All rights reserved.

Dedication

*To Jane Brostrom Lewis,
whose spousal love, listening ears, keen eyes, and unimaginable patience
gave me life to enable the writing of this book.*

*To the Reverend Mary Luck Stanley,
Spouse, Mother, Priest, Author, and my late Sister,
whose encouragement led to the publication of this book.*

*To the congregations I have been part of as a lay person, seminarian, and
priest, all of whom have informed this book:
St. Mark's Church, Philadelphia, Pennsylvania, 1955–58
The Church of Our Merciful Savior, Kaufman, Texas, 1958–61
St. Alban's Church, Arlington, Texas, 1961–67
St. Anselm's Canterbury House, Arlington, Texas, 1961–67
St. William Laud Church, Pittsburg, Texas, 1967–69
St. John's Church, Dallas, Texas, 1969–81
St. Stephen's Church, Sherman, Texas, 1974–78
The Church of St. Martin-in-the-Fields, London, England, 1977
The Chapel of Christ the King, University of London, 1977
Grace Church, Madison, Wisconsin, 1979
St. Francis House, University of Wisconsin–Madison, 1979–81
The Church of the Annunciation, Waukegan, Illinois, 1979–81
The Church of the Epiphany, Richardson, Texas, 1980–83
St. John's Church, Portsmouth, New Hampshire, 1983–86
The Church of the Redeemer, Rochester, New Hampshire, 1986–91
Durham Cathedral, England, 1987
The Church of Saint Mary the Virgin, Falmouth, Maine, 1991–2004
St. Paul's Cathedral, Syracuse, New York, 2004–14
St. Barnabas Church, Fredericksburg, Texas, 2015–19
The Church of the Ascension, Montell, Texas, 2017–19
St. Martin's Church, Mason, Texas, 2016–present*

Now the Lord is the Spirit, and where the Spirit of the Lord is, there is freedom. And all of us, with unveiled faces, seeing the glory of the Lord as though reflected in a mirror, are being transformed into the same image from one degree of glory to another, for this comes from the Lord, the Spirit. —2 CORINTHIANS 3:17–18

Table of Contents

Illustrations and Tables | ix
Preface and Acknowledgments: The Journey of This Book | xi
Introduction: Participation in God's Glory:
  Taken, Blessed, Broken, and Given | xxi

Chapter 1: Coming to Faith: Human Desire and Longing for God in Community, Implanted by God | 3

Chapter 2: Participation in God in the New Testament | 17

Chapter 3: Coming to Faith and Praising God | 28

Chapter 4: Baptism and Eucharist | 39

Chapter 5: Adaptive Change as Participation in God | 60

Postscript: Taste and See That the Lord Is Good! | 78

Bibliography | 81
Name/Subject Index | 87
Scripture Index | 95

Illustrations and Tables

Figures

1. Old Testament Trinity, Andrei Rublev, ca. 1400s | 1
2. Distinguishing Technical Problems and Adaptive Challenges | 62
3. Leadership from a Position of Authority | 63
4. Self-Transforming Mind | 64
5. Productive Zone of Disequilibrium | 71
6. Maundy Thursday Liturgy, St. Paul's Church, Syracuse, New York, 2015 | 80

Preface and Acknowledgments
The Journey of This Book

I HAVE BEEN BLESSED by many chance encounters and relationships. I acknowledge that many if not most of these encounters were made possible because of straight, white, male privilege, of which I am a beneficiary. Partly because I have children and grandchildren who are women in the professions, a son-in-law and grandchildren who are Black, and family members of multiple generations who are LGBTQ+, I am more mindful of my privilege than would otherwise be the case. My late sister, the Reverend Mary Luck Stanley, coauthored a book with three other ordained women, *Grace in the Rearview Mirror*, that told stories of the challenges that they faced and it too reveals the privilege I have had.

My first teacher in all matters of church was my father, the late Reverend Canon George E. Luck. My debt to him is beyond my comprehension. Dad's primary mentor was the Reverend Dr. Thomas J. Tally, who was rector of St. Barnabas Church in Denton, Texas, while Dad was a student at the University of North Texas. Father Tally went on to become one of the preeminent liturgical scholars in the world. He and I stayed in touch, and after he died, I attended his funeral at Holy Cross Monastery in West Park, New York. His last words to me were, "Give 'em heaven!"

The Reverend Michael Merriman was a young priest leading diocesan youth ministry in the Diocese of Dallas when we met. I was a camper at Camp Crucis in Granbury, Texas. His years of leading conferences at Camp Crucis, where we experimented with

Preface and Acknowledgments

many kinds of liturgies, broke open for me how engaging and exciting community-based liturgy can be. And it was Michael Merriman, through a series of recordings by Michael Marshall, who introduced me to the framework of the three bodies of Christ being taken, blessed, broken, and given—in Jesus himself, in the bread of the Eucharist, and in Christ's body, the church. In my senior year of high school we were cochairs of the Division of Youth in the Diocese of Dallas. Michael went on to become canon precentor at Grace Cathedral in San Francisco, executive director of Associated Parishes for Liturgy and Mission, and author of a popular book on the catechumenate.

In my junior year at Austin College I was allowed to participate in the London study abroad program run by Central College of Pella, Iowa. I was considering a vocation to the priesthood and the confluence of numerous chance meetings and experiences in England truly changed the course of my life. Upon arriving in London, Michael Stone, a friend from Camp Crucis, was studying for the priesthood at King's College, London. He absolutely insisted that I become involved as a volunteer social worker in the Social Service Unit at the Church of St. Martin-in-the-Fields—against almost all of the reasons I wanted to be in London. The ministry of that place was to the homeless people of London, providing counseling, tokens for transportation and meals, food that could be prepared and eaten on the street, and refuge from the winter elements. One of my tasks was to review index cards with information about each guest and, if it had been six months since their last visit, to put their index card in the "dead file." I could not help but read many of the notes on the cards, and I realized that there is a thin line for all of us between being able to take care of ourselves and becoming dependent on the care of others and that almost always it was simply a matter of life circumstances—a lost job, a failed relationship, addiction, or other mental health issues. This was a profound learning experience for a twenty-one year old from suburban Dallas, Texas.

Through a totally coincidental gathering following a Sunday liturgy at Rochester Cathedral on my first Sunday in England I was given contact information for the Reverend Dr. Eric Mascall, the leading Anglican Thomist of the twentieth century. Under his guidance I did an independent study on the problem of evil in the writing of Thomas Aquinas, a study made much more relevant due to my work at St. Martin's.

One week-long break I went to York and was delighted to find that the preacher at the cathedral on that Sunday was going to be the Right Reverend and Right Honorable Lord Michael Ramsey, retired Archbishop of Canterbury. I had heard much about Ramsey from Michael Merriman, who years earlier had coincidentally met Lady Joan Ramsey on the tube in London while Ramsey was Archbishop, and who invited Michael to drop by Lambeth Palace, which he did. As I attended the daily offices at York Minster a young nun, Sister Anne, was also attending the offices, and she introduced herself to me. When I told her how excited I was to hear Ramsey preach she said, "You'll have to meet him!" to which I said, "Yes, and then I'll meet the queen when I return to London!" Sunday came, Ramsey preached a brilliant sermon, and then there was a reception. At the reception Ramsey, who had been Archbishop of York before Canterbury, made his way around the room and greeted people he knew, often with hugs and kisses. When he was done, he scanned the room and Sister Anne said to me, "Go meet him!" I didn't dare budge. Suddenly there was a strong shove in the small of my back, and as I stumbled forward, I looked up to realize Ramsey had seen the whole thing. As I looked up at him, he was smiling at me and holding out his arms to catch me. We spoke of my discernment about ordination, and I asked whether it would be good to study in England. Ramsey said some study in England would be fine, but that as an American I should go to a seminary of the Episcopal Church since "we really are two different churches." When I asked if he had a recommendation, he said that Nashotah House was kind enough to invite him every year or two to be a visiting professor. I knew Nashotah because Dad did summer graduate work there and I had spent several summers there as a child. I floated out of the reception and went back to London. Thank you, Sister Anne, for the shove in the back.

On Sundays in London I usually attended the Chapel of Christ the King of the University of London. The head chaplain, the Reverend Victor Stock, and the whole team there were theologically classically Anglican, politically progressive, and had a liturgical style I would describe as deconstructed and socially relevant Anglo-Catholic. In particular, the Holy Week liturgies were interactive and powerful, and they still shape all of my thinking about Holy Week.

Back at Austin College, I was still in discernment about ordination when I took two courses in the spring semester of my senior year that particularly led me to feel called to enter the ordination process. First, following up on my semester in London I took a seminar on Tudor history from Dr. A. J. Carlson, who often referred to his colleague from doctoral study at Princeton University, Dr. John Booty. Dr. John Booty was professor of church history at Episcopal Divinity School and was editing the work of Richard Hooker for the Folger Shakespeare Library, from which I quote in this book. The proudest moment of my undergraduate years was when Dr. Carlson referred to me as "our young Anglican scholar."

Simultaneously, I took a course in cognitive psychology, taught by Dr. Karen Nelson, a recent graduate of the Harvard School of Education. The first day of class she introduced us to the moral development theories of Lawrence Kohlberg, who taught at Harvard. I had studied philosophical ethics the previous semester. Here in front of my eyes were the various ways of doing ethics I had learned the previous semester but arranged developmentally. I was grabbed! I was considering making this my life's work when, one Sunday back home at St. John's in Dallas, I realized that perhaps the best place where this sort of development takes place is the church. At that point I began the ordination process, and my term paper was about how the liturgies of Holy Week encourage the kind or moral development that Kohlberg describes.

I arrived at Nashotah House in the fall of 1978. No one there had heard of Lawrence Kohlberg. The ordination of women had been approved two years earlier, and all of the faculty supported it. The Book of Common Prayer 1979 was approved by the General Convention while I was in seminary, and one of the leading contributors was our professor of liturgy, the Reverend Dr. Louis

Preface and Acknowledgments

Weil. Louis had gone to SMU in Dallas and had been confirmed at the Canterbury House there with my mom. From Louis I learned that in the early church the Eucharist was a full meal. From Louis I learned about the centrality of holy baptism in the whole theological approach of the 1979 prayer book. But more than that, Louis was my advisor and he would have all of his advisees to his house for a communal meal with the Eucharist at his dining room table. Further, I had the honor of being his faculty assistant for three years during which we talked often. All of this is irreplaceable.

Also in my first year the Reverend Ruth Tiffany Barnhouse, MD, Episcopal priest, and psychiatrist, came to Nashotah as a visiting lecturer. She gave a presentation on the spiritual exercises of Saint Ignatius. As she spoke, I found myself thinking of how it overlapped in some ways with Kohlberg. I had a chance to ask her about this and she replied, "Yes. But more like Kohlberg is James Fowler. Kohlberg teaches at the Harvard School of Education and Fowler teaches at Harvard Divinity School, but they had common students who said they should talk. They did, and Fowler has just published a little book where he has modified Kohlberg to something he calls "faith development." The book is called *Life Maps*. You should get it!" I did, and I spent the rest of my time in seminary trying to integrate it into many papers. Years later I learned that Ruth had been the psychiatrist of Sylvia Plath, whose poetry I had read for a course in London. Ramsey did come to Nashotah my second and third years to teach Anglican Theology. He took walks every day around Nashotah Lake with a student, one on one; after I joined him for one of these walks, we began a correspondence that lasted until he was no longer able to write. In a series of talks for a retreat on the transfiguration Ramsey introduced me to the theological notion of human transformation into the image of Christ, particularly referencing 2 Cor 3:18. This gave my cognitive psychological understanding of human development a theological foundation. Ramsey attended a birthday party for me and gave me a book of pen and ink drawings of Durham, England, where he and Joan lived at that time.

Two years after I graduated from Nashotah House I moved from Texas to Portsmouth, New Hampshire. I poked around

Harvard Divinity School and found that they had a program called Ministers in the Vicinity that allowed local clergy to take courses for credit at only half of the tuition. I took a course, Faith and Its Transformations Across the Life Span, taught by Sharon Parks, who did her doctoral work under James Fowler, who had himself left Harvard for Emory University to live near his parents. But Fowler did a guest lectures and we were able to talk. Sharon allowed me to roam freely in my papers trying to integrate theology, liturgy, and faith development.

In Portsmouth I was curate of St. John's, whose rector, the Reverend Gordon Allen, was English, and he had studied for the priesthood at Durham University. He had a classmate, the Venerable Derek Hodgson, who was an archdeacon of the Diocese of Durham and a canon at Durham Cathedral where he lived in the Cathedral Close. After I had moved from Portsmouth to be rector of the Church of the Redeemer in Rochester, New Hampshire, Derek approached Gordon about doing a clergy exchange. Gordon went to England every year anyway to see family and wondered if I would be interested. At this time the Church of England was not ordaining women, and I was concerned about taking advantage of something my women colleagues in New Hampshire could not. I talked with a number of them, and the consensus response was, "First, thanks for asking. Because you did, I trust you to go to England and talk about what a gift the ordination of women is. Go!" I did go, and I did talk much about my sisters in the priesthood.

My next-door neighbor in Durham was the Reverend Dan Hardy, the Van Mildert Professor of Divinity at Durham University at the time, the same post Michael Ramsey had once held. Dan and his wife were very hospitable and generous with their time. They were both Americans, but Dan had studied at Oxford and was the father-in-law of Dr. David Ford, a theologian at Cambridge. Through Dan's tutelage I became a student in the master of letters in theology program at Durham, with hopes of eventually entering the PhD program. British postgraduate programs are research based with little to no coursework. I lived in America where I did the research and writing. I would send my written work via the post to Dan. He would critique it, and then I would write some more. It was slow going, and we did have occasional transatlantic phone calls to expedite the process. With Dan's encouragement, I worked on a theology of parish ministry, something Dan said almost no one was doing or cared about doing. A few years later I went back to Durham for a sabbatical, and we made great progress. Unfortunately for me, soon after that Dan came back to the United States to be the director of the Center of Theological Inquiry in Princeton. True to Dan's assessment, no one else at Durham was interested in my project and so I was done with the program. But the idea of doing critical theological work on congregational life would not leave me.

By this time I was rector of Saint Mary the Virgin in Falmouth, Maine, and was eligible for a sabbatical. But I had three children at home, lived in a rectory on the church grounds, and going away for three months was not really feasible. Instead we agreed to a "flex sabbatical" that allowed me to take one or two courses each semester at Harvard while continuing to be a full-time rector. In looking at the options at Harvard I came across the Harvard Extension School. It is the best kept secret of Harvard University. Begun in the nineteenth century, originally as a night school for people who had been unable to go to college, it now offers associate, bachelor, and master of liberal arts degree programs that are full Harvard degrees. Graduates go on to graduate and professional schools across the country, including at Harvard. There are no admissions requirements to take courses. After three courses one may apply for a degree program, and once admitted to a degree program, one is eligible to take any courses that are offered at Harvard University. More than one person has said something along the lines of, "Contrary to popular perception, at the extension school you don't have to have a brilliant record to get into Harvard, but you have to work hard to stay in."

The extension school accepted my courses from the divinity school. My first extension school course was Comparative Religious Ethics, taught by Charles Hallisey. When I entered the classroom, I realized that the vast majority of the students were recent immigrants who were working full time and taking classes at night at Harvard. These people are my heroes. In the course we studied Hindu, Jewish, Islamic, and Christian ethics. This class introduced me to the Jewish theologian, Rabbi Joseph Soloveitchik, whose work figures prominently in this book. Some years later, after writing a required entrance paper and having a one-on-one interview, the Reverend Dr. Sarah Coakley kindly allowed me to be the only master's degree student in her doctoral seminar on the Trinity at the divinity school. Paul Hanson's course Religion and Politics taught me that the founders of our country were fearful of a Puritan theocracy, but they also believed that another reason for disestablishment was to allow religious leaders to critique the government. Harvey Cox's course The Future of the World Religions allowed my small group on religion and science to have several meetings with senior faculty at the Harvard Smithsonian Center for Astrophysics, the best place ever to discuss cosmology and the possibility of God. My thanks to Paul Hanson who served as the advisor for my master's thesis, "The Breaking of the Bread: the Gospels and the Millennium Development Goals."

While I was studying part time at Harvard, I was also a participant in and then chaplain for the Clergy Leadership Project, which took place at Trinity Conference Center in West Cornwall, Connecticut. Wendy Denn was director of the Trinity Conference Center, and the coordinator of the program. Out of all the people I have known, I think she is the most brilliant, with a thorough grasp of everything theological and organizational, all focusing on hospitality, a central theme in this book. Through that program I was introduced to Josh Ruxin of the Earth Institute at Columbia who taught about the UN Millennium Development Goals. Most importantly, Hugh O'Doherty of the Kennedy School of Government at Harvard, a colleague of Ron Heifetz, taught on the subject of adaptive change and leadership, which is the focus of the final chapter. Wendy also introduced the practice of mindful eating and drinking, which improved my quality of life immensely, and which I use today in my work guiding food and wine pairings as a wine advisor. See the postscript of this book for more. Thank you, Wendy!

Preface and Acknowledgments

While I was dean and rector of St. Paul's Cathedral in Syracuse, I again became eligible for a sabbatical, and again we agreed to a flex sabbatical that allowed me to be in the doctor of ministry program in congregational development at Bexley Seabury Seminary in Chicago.

My largest debt of gratitude, and most important acknowledgment, is to the Rev. Dr. Jason Fout, associate professor of Anglican theology at Bexley Seabury and the coeditor of the Anglican Theological Review. I wanted Jason to be my dissertation director because I not only wanted someone who is knowledgeable but someone who would bring real rigor to an exercise I hoped would become the foundation for this book. And irony of ironies, Jason did his PhD dissertation at Cambridge University under Dan Hardy, to whom Jason's first book is dedicated. Jason helped me in countless ways to add content and wrap the package I began under Dan decades earlier.

This work will develop a particular theology of participation in the life of God, and describe how this theology of participation in God informs individual and congregational development. What is often missing in congregational development discourse is a theological framework. The subject of congregational development is human beings and their relationships with God and each other. This theological framework provides individual and congregational development with an answer to the question, What does individual and congregational development have to do with God? Much of the reading and writing for this book were done during the COVID-19 pandemic, which raised new questions about how Christian communities gather without being in person. This in turn has prompted new questions and thoughts about the nature of worship, ecclesiology, and adaptive challenges—questions which I will address through a theology of participation in God, particularly, participation in God's glory.

There are many fingerprints on the text of this book. Any deficiencies are the fault of the author alone.

Introduction

*Participation in God's Glory:
Taken, Blessed, Broken, Given*

From ancient times in Jewish tradition until current practice in Christianity, bread is taken, blessed, broken, and given. This simple practice has its origins in household meals where it still takes place and in vast cathedrals attended by thousands. These actions with bread are also patterns in human community when people gather at table; they are taken and held by God in a common space around a table, receive blessing by God's Word and Sacrament and one another in community, are broken and dispersed when the gathering ends, and then given and sent out into the world by God to carry out God's mission and ministry. In this pattern individuals and the gathered community both receive and offer.

Those gathered are not merely static or empty vessels needing filling. Each person comes to the gathering within a particular life context of family history, ethnicity, race, economic life, gender identity, geographical influences, and unique personalities. Yet all have in common that they are in the midst of living within the paradox of being a human, of being made in the image and likeness of God, and yet also struggling to fulfill being in the image and likeness of God—and even struggling to understand what that means. Being made in the image and likeness of God places human beings as integrally part of creation, which is God's first gift and is the foundation of participating in God's life by simply dwelling in creation. Yet to be human is to not only dwell in creation but to be like God in creation.

God incarnate in Jesus Christ was also such a human being with a particular family history, ethnicity, race, gender identity, geographical influence, and unique personality. Where Jesus is most unique is that he perfectly fulfilled the image and likeness of God in his life and ministry. In his own life he was taken and held in the womb of his mother Mary and the in arms of Mary and Joseph. He was blessed in his baptism by John the Baptist and his transfiguration on the mount. He submitted his life to betrayal, torture, and the ultimate brokenness of death on a cross. In his resurrection back into the complexities of human life he gave his life to all and breathed his spirit into his disciples so that they and we are now his body.

Through our participation in table fellowship, at home and in wider communities, we are transformed from one degree of glory to another; we become like God in Jesus Christ as we are taken, blessed, broken, and given, participating in the transforming power of the Holy Spirit, as we strive to fulfill God's mission and ministry in the world.

Congregational development therefore is about the spiritual transformation of individuals within community and the transformation of the community working together as individuals. Thus, congregational development is about participating in the life of the Trinity of God, as many persons but one being, the body of Christ.

FIGURE 1

Old Testament Trinity, Andrei Rublev, ca. 1400s

CHAPTER 1

Coming to Faith

*Human Desire and Longing
for God in Community, Implanted by God*

THE HEBREW SCRIPTURES REVEAL that it is impossible to talk about humanity without talking about God, and just as importantly, it is impossible to talk about God without talking about humanity. This chapter will introduce the notion of the "two *adams*" as reflected in the two creation stories in the book of Genesis. In the NRSVue translation, in the two creation stories, the word "humans" in Gen 1:26 and the word "Adam" in Gen 2:7 are translations of the one Hebrew word *adam*, pronounced ah-dahm, which means "human." Later in Gen 2:23 we find the first explicitly gendered terms applied to humans, *ish* for male and *ishah* for female.[1] In what follows, the word *adam* conforms to the Hebrew text of both creation stories, and in every case, adam refers to all of humanity generally. For consistency of carrying this theme of adam, when I quote an author who practices the now antiquated use of the words "man" or "mankind" I have inserted the word "adam."

Also, for the purposes of this book, it is important to note that adam includes all races, genders, and sexual orientations of people. Certainly, all early characters in the Hebrew Scriptures had skin that was black or brown, as did Jesus. I mention this here to

---

1. SBL, *Study Bible*, 282.

break apart any image we may have in our minds that to be fully human or a "normal" human or to be like Jesus implies any particular race, gender, or sexual orientation. Indeed, when it comes to the race of people, the only race the Bible is concerned with is the human race.

Soloveitchik refers to "two Adams," "Adam the first" and "Adam the second."[2] The two adams capture the dichotomy of human life: on one hand, the human desire to be like God, and on the other hand, the human desire to experience freedom, while also experiencing the human desire for community. Both adams have a certain glory, and yet these glories themselves live in tension. Adam the first has the glory of being made in the image and likeness of God, which gives human beings the gift of moral agency that is unique among the creatures of earth. Adam the second has the glory of redemption, compassion, and love, which are how humans exercise the agency they are given, such that God's own glory is lived out in human beings. The adaptive challenge of adam the first is to exercise the agency of being made in God's image and likeness by embracing compassion and love, a self emptying of glory for glory. The adaptive challenge of adam the second is to embrace the uniquely human power and glory of agency and rationality in adam the first, in order to have the power to exercise agency in compassion and love. Adam the first asks adam the second, What is the good of having compassion and love without power to accomplish them? And adam the second asks adam the first, What is the good of having power if it is not used for compassion and love? The dialogical dance of the two adams leads to glorification, not glorification of humanity but glorification of God, from one degree of glory to another.

Nahum Sarna maintains that the Hebrew Bible is both God-centered and Israel-centered. Genesis says that the entire human race is endowed with free will, with agency. Humans are charged with moral responsibility and inescapable accountability, and humanity is a single family whose ultimate destiny is determined by

---

2. Soloveitchik, *Lonely*, 10.

God.[3] In the Hebrew Scriptures, the human creature is bound to its Creator, God. There is in adam a God-given sense of desire for a relationship with the Creator. The Hebrew Scriptures are in many ways a series of stories and teachings not only about the relationship but about how adam fulfills its desire for a relationship with the Creator. There are ways to have a good and true relationship with the Creator, and there are bad ways as well.

The book of Genesis proclaims that God is the Creator of the universe. Sarna translates Gen 1:26, "And God said, 'Let us make [adam] in our image, after our likeness. They shall rule the fish of the sea, the birds of the sky, the cattle, the whole earth, and all creeping things that creep upon the earth.'" God has put humanity in charge of God's creatures in God's stead. God creates and then puts humanity in charge.[4] In doing so, this is the primary way God calls humanity to participate in God's life, by exercising godlike dominion in creation. The dominion humanity has of creation gives humans power within creation, be it power to sustain creation and care for creation or power to destroy and exploit creation. God giving humanity this power within creation is to make humans godlike, and at the same time, for humanity to serve God's purpose, humans must exercise dominion on God's terms. Humans have been given the freedom to exercise agency, yet to use this freedom contrary to God's purpose is to become enslaved to the whims and shortsightedness of thought humans suffer when God's will is ignored or denied. The irony is that God made all of creation good, including humanity, and that God only wills goodness for the creatures made in God's image and likeness. In rebelling against God, humanity ultimately rebels against our own creatureliness, our own humanity.

Humans are the only creatures who are given moral agency, but this agency is granted by God to act as God's agents. When humans act as agents of ourselves, we are at enmity with God, with one another, and thus, with our own selves. The book of Deuteronomy says that God commands us to love God "so that it may

---

3. Sarna, *Genesis*, xii.
4. Sarna, *Genesis*, 11.

go well with you . . . in a land flowing with milk and honey, as the LORD, the God of your ancestors, has promised you. Hear, O Israel: The LORD is our God, the LORD alone. You shall love the LORD your God with all your heart, and with all your soul, and with all your might."[5]

As Joseph Soloveitchik observes, the two stories of creation describe the dilemma of humankind—what he describes as a contradiction in human nature—intentionally contained within the book of Genesis. For Soloveitchik the two stories represent two different versions of adam, not adam as a particular human being but adam as prototype of all humanity. Soloveitchik is mindful that the two stories have different sources but sees that there is more at work than source theory.

> It is, of course, true that the two accounts of the creation of Adam differ considerably. This incongruity was not discovered by the Bible critics. Our sages of old were aware of it. However, the answer lies not in an alleged dual tradition but in dual Adam, not in an imaginary contradiction between two versions but in a real contradiction in the nature of Adam. The two accounts deal with two Adams, two Adams, two types, two representatives of humanity, and it is no wonder that they are not identical.[6]

Sarna also observes a dual nature in humankind. Humans "enjoy a unique relationship to God, who communicates with them alone." Yet, that humans are created in the universe after the creation of all the other animals "focuses attention on the dual nature of humankind, the creatureliness and earthiness as well as the godlike qualities."[7] This is the paradox of humanity. We are made in God's image and likeness, and yet, being like God is the very thing that we rebel against. We want to not only be like God but to be like God on our terms, which means we want to be God. When we fail to be who God created us to be, we are not merely being

---

5. Deut 6:3–5.
6. Soloveitchik, *Lonely*, 9.
7. Sarna, *Genesis*, 11.

disobedient to God; we are failing ourselves as well. We as a species of creatures are the ones who suffer the consequences of our rebellion. Creation may be subject to humanity, but humanity is subject to God. As Jason Fout observes, "The shape of human life in light of this glory is obedience: joyful obedience, loving obedience, free obedience.... The relation of the human creature to the superabundant, gracious, glorious God is obedience."[8]

The way that we participate in the divine life of God is to embrace our particular role as creatures who are human, the only creatures God has brought into the most intimate relationship between God and all of God's creatures. By serving as God's agents in creation, humans reflect the glory of God. God's most glorious creature reflects God's glory in the very act of exercising dominion, in accordance with God's commandments in both creation stories of Genesis. The verbs in the passages from Genesis that follow describe the human place in creation: be fruitful, multiply, fill, subdue, have dominion, till, keep, toil, eat.

> God blessed them, and God said to them, "Be fruitful and multiply and fill the earth and subdue it and have dominion over the fish of the sea and over the birds of the air and over every living thing that moves upon the earth." God said, "See, I have given you every plant yielding seed that is upon the face of all the earth and every tree with seed in its fruit; you shall have them for food. And to every beast of the earth and to every bird of the air and to everything that creeps on the earth, everything that has the breath of life, I have given every green plant for food." And it was so. God saw everything that he had made, and indeed, it was very good. And there was evening and there was morning, the sixth day.[9]
>
> The LORD God took the [adam] and put him in the garden of Eden to till it and keep it. And the LORD God commanded the [adam], "You may freely eat of every tree of the garden, but of the tree of the knowledge of

---

8. Fout, *Fully Alive*, loc. 96.
9. Gen 1:28–31.

good and evil you shall not eat, for in the day that you eat of it you shall die."[10]

> Because you have listened to the voice of your wife and have eaten of the tree about which I commanded you, "You shall not eat of it," cursed is the ground because of you; in toil you shall eat of it all the days of your life; thorns and thistles it shall bring forth for you; and you shall eat the plants of the field. By the sweat of your face you shall eat bread until you return to the ground, for out of it you were taken; you are dust, and to dust you shall return.[11]

To the degree that the verbs in the above passages may at first appear to be in conflict or, at a minimum, to be in tension, they reflect the dual nature of humanity. Humans exist as God's agents in creation, thus exercising dominion in it but always under the ultimate dominion of God who made humans out of the very stuff of creation. Contrariwise, when humans deny their role in creation and try to put themselves in the place of God, they do not reflect God's glory but instead reveal human shame.

Soloveitchik makes the claim that living in this paradox leaves human beings with a feeling of loneliness and that this loneliness is the source of human longing, both longing for God and longing for community. But for Soloveitchik, human loneliness is also about loneliness from oneself. Basing his analysis on the two creation stories of Genesis, he lays out two versions of humanity, both of which are true and paradoxical. It is this very paradox that causes humans to be lonely from themselves.

> Both Adams want to be human. Both strive to be themselves, to be what God commanded them to be, namely, Adam. . . . The incongruity of methods is, therefore, a result not of diverse objectives but of diverse interpretive approaches to the one objective they both pursue. The two Adams do not concur in their interpretations of this objective. The idea of humanity, the great challenge

10. Gen 2:15–17.
11. Gen 3:17–19.

summoning Adam to action and movement, is placed by them in two incommensurate perspectives. While Adam the first wants to reclaim himself from a closed-in, non-reflective, natural existence by setting himself up as a dignified majestic being capable of ruling his environment, Adam the second sees his separateness from nature and his existential uniqueness not in dignity or majesty but in something else. There is, in his opinion, another mode of existence through which Adam can find his own self, namely, the redemptive, which is not necessarily identical with the dignified.[12]

Soloveitchik bases his paradigms of the two adams on four primary discrepancies in the two stories.

The first creation story says that adam was created in the image and likeness of God but says nothing about how the body was formed. The second story says that adam was created from the dust of the ground and became a living being when God breathed the breath of life into adam's nostrils. Second, adam the first was given a mandate to fill the earth and subdue it, while adam the second was charged with keeping the garden and cultivating it. Third, in the first story males and females are created concurrently, while in the second story the male is created first and the female is created to be a helpmate. Fourth, in the first creation story God's name is Elohim, while in the second story both Elohim and YHWH are used. For Soloveitchik this means that

> *Adam* the first who was fashioned in the image of God was blessed with great drive for creative activity and immeasurable resources for the realization of this goal, the most outstanding of which is the intelligence, the human mind, capable of confronting the outside world and inquiring into its complex workings.... *Adam* the first is interested in just a single aspect of reality and asks one question only—"How does the cosmos function?" He is not fascinated by the question, "Why does the cosmos function at all?" nor is he interested in the question, "What is its essence?" He is only curious to know how

---

12. Soloveitchik, *Lonely*, 21.

it works. In fact, even this "how" question with which *Adam* the first is preoccupied is limited in scope. He is concerned not with the question per se, but with its practical implications. He raises not a metaphysical but a practical, technical "how" question. To be precise, his question is related not to the genuine functioning of the cosmos in itself but to the possibility of reproducing the dynamics of the cosmos by employing quantified-mathematized media which *Adam* evolves through postulation and creative thinking.... In other words, Adam is a dignified being and to be human means to live with dignity.... Hence, *Adam* the first is aggressive, bold, and victory-minded. His motto is success, triumph over the cosmic forces. He engages in creative work, trying to imitate his Maker (*imitatio Dei*).[13]

This view of adam contrasts rather sharply with adam the second.

> Instead his inquiry is of a metaphysical nature and a threefold one. He wants to know: "Why is it?" "What is it?" "Who is it?" (1) He wonders: "Why did the world in its totality come into existence? Why is *Adam* confronted by this stupendous and indifferent order of things and events?" (2) He asks: "What is the purpose of all this? What is the message that is embedded in organic and inorganic matter, and what does the great challenge reaching me from beyond the fringes of the universe as well as from the depths of my tormented soul mean?" (3) *Adam* the second keeps on wondering: "Who is the One who trails me steadily, uninvited and unwanted, like an everlasting shadow, and vanishes into the recesses of transcendence the very instant I turn around to confront this numinous, awesome, and mysterious 'One'? Who is the One who fills *Adam* with awe and bliss, humility and a sense of greatness, concurrently? Who is the One to whom *Adam* clings in passionate, all-consuming love and from whom he flees in mortal fear and dread? Who is the One who fascinates *Adam* irresistibly and at the same time rejects him irrevocably? Who is the One whom *Adam* experiences both as the *mysterium tremendum*

---

13. Soloveitchik, *Lonely*, 12–16.

and as the most elementary, most obvious, and most understandable truth? Who is the One who is *deus revelatus* and *deus absconditus* simultaneously? Who is the One whose life-giving and life-warming breath *Adam* feels constantly and who at the same time remains distant and remote from all?"[14]

The attempt to reconcile the two adams in oneself leads to a loneliness where, at one and the same time, one sees one's own unique creatureliness among all the creatures, one's own uniqueness from all other humans, and yet also sees connection to the whole of creation and to all other humans. Out of this loneliness adam longs for knowledge and relationship with God in order to understand everything else that can be known.

Adam has a longing for the experience of transcendent God, as do all individual humans as children of adam. The challenge is to find the authentic means to that experience. Life presents many tempting shortcuts to adam the first; power, many and varied addictions, and unhealthy relationships are but a few examples. The Hebrew Scriptures are full of stories where people tried to experience God by their own efforts. Everyone, from high-level executives to homeless people on the street know this longing and eventually learn the shortcuts. Sometimes the failure to experience true God in the shortcut becomes obvious, and often the response is to try more shortcuts. Adam the first is oriented to keep trying to experience God by thinking that they have the means to achieve godlike transcendence. Adam the second realizes total dependence on God and knows that love, redemption, and forgiveness of oneself by God and loving, redeeming, and forgiving others is at the heart of God's transcendent life.

Even more, adam longs for God in order to have a sense that oneself is known by God, despite the limitations of the ability to know God. It becomes more important for adam to have faith that oneself is known by God, than to have a false sense that one can know God. This is when adam realizes that life itself is a gift not of

---

14. Soloveitchik, *Lonely*, 20–21.

one's own choosing but of God, and that participation in human life within God's creation is itself a participation in the life of God.

And yet, the act of faith creates its own kind of loneliness. It is not satisfied by work companions or family life or any other human gathering. It only begins to be addressed when humans gather with other humans who also have faith in God.

> There, not only hands are joined, but experiences as well; there, one hears not only the rhythmic sound of the production line, but also the rhythmic beat of hearts starved for existential companionship and all-embracing sympathy and experiencing the grandeur of the faith commitment; there, one lonely soul finds another soul tormented by loneliness and solitude yet unqualifiedly committed. . . . Thus, in crisis and distress there was planted the seed of a new type of community—the faith community which reached full fruition in the covenant between God and Abraham.[15]

In light of Soloveitchik's point, I will turn to the story of Sarah and Abraham, the first community of faith, in order to explore how the two adams came to be reconciled in their faith by showing compassion, revealing God's glory in human agency. The paradox of the two adams is that to be human, adam must always live in the tension between adam the first and adam the second. Both are valid, both are essential to humanity, and they are dependent on each other for fulfillment. It is not the case that one defeats or prevails over the other, for to do so would be to deny an essential aspect of humanity. Rather, they actually need each other for the other to thrive. In the story of Sarah and Abraham the two adams are reconciled and fulfilled.

Beginning in chapter 12 of the book of Genesis, Abram and Sarai (before God bestows new names) are given two significant or corresponding promises by God: the gift of land and the gift of heirs. For the next five chapters of Genesis, functioning in the nature of adam the first, they take many steps on their sojourn to

---

15. Soloveitchik, *Lonely*, 40.

have God's promise fulfilled. This history leads to a poignant and even ironic story in chapter 18.

Sarah and Abraham (as they are now named) have spent their lives wandering and hearing God's promise of land and progeny over and over. Abraham has expressed frustration and impatience with God. "The story of their lives is the story of hopeful but impatient groaning as they wait for the redemption of their bodies and of their history."[16] Abraham and Sarah are encamped, and it is during the heat of the day. Abraham sees what appears to be three people standing near him, and he runs to them and bows down before them. Thinking that they are human wanderers as Abraham and Sarah are, Abraham and Sarah offer them hospitality. But the reader knows from the first verse that the Lord is present in these three visitors. Abraham beseeches the visitors to stay for refreshment. And he offers to bring them water, to wash their feet, and to give them rest under the shade of a tree. But in exercising extravagant hospitality Abraham and Sarah exceed the promise they have made. Instead, Sarah prepares cakes of bread. A calf is roasted, and milk and curds are served.

> Unlike the previous theophanies, this one is not accompanied by an act of worship or the building of an altar; in actual fact, hospitality to strangers itself becomes an act of worship. As the Talmud puts it, "Hospitality to wayfarers is greater than welcoming the Divine Presence." . . . Abraham's openhearted, liberal hospitality to the total strangers knows no bounds. . . . He promises to fetch "a morsel of bread" but prepares a lavish feast. The Talmud remarks, "Such is the way of the righteous; they promise little but perform much." In asking Sarah to bake cakes, Abraham specifies the use of "choice flour," that is, the finest and choicest of wheat flour, the type from which meal offerings were later brought to the sanctuary. He himself selects the calf for the main dish, a rare delicacy and a sign of princely hospitality among pastoralists. He provides curds and milk, the basic products of a pastoral economy. Curds are the coagulated state of the fatty part

---

16. Brueggemann, *Genesis*, loc. 158.

of the milk, corresponding to the modern *leben* or yogurt. Milk was highly esteemed in the ancient Near East and was offered to the gods. It was regarded as a source of vitality and possessor of curative powers. Abraham personally serves the strangers this rich fare and stands close by, ready to attend to their needs.[17]

Unbeknownst to them, Abraham and Sarah are about to have their dream fulfilled by virtue of their hospitality to strangers.

One of the strangers says, "I will surely return to you in due season, and your wife Sarah shall have a son." Sarah, listening in the tent entrance laughs and says, "After I have grown old, and my husband is old, shall I have pleasure?"[18] But as promised, "The LORD dealt with Sarah as he had said, and the LORD did for Sarah as he had promised. Sarah conceived and bore Abraham a son in his old age, at the time of which God had spoken to him. . . . Now Sarah said, 'God has brought laughter for me; everyone who hears will laugh with me.' And she said, 'Who would ever have said to Abraham that Sarah would nurse children? Yet I have borne him a son in his old age.'"[19]

In Soloveitchik's terms, Abraham and Sarah have reconciled adam the first and adam the second, largely because their adam the first ambitions became adam the second ambitions—they engaged in humble service towards others and in doing so served God. Abraham and Sarah moved to service as true worship, offering hospitality to strangers, and in doing so truly surrendered to God. They, for at least a moment, forgot themselves and their quest, and focused on serving others, exhibiting the essence of faith. They used their adam the first power, wealth, and knowledge to serve their adam the second purpose of serving others. They exhibited that true faith happens when one's will and actions move from serving one's own interests and desires to serving others, having faith enough in God to offer hospitality to others. They had faith enough to give precious, expensive food to total strangers. And in

---

17. Sarna, *Genesis*, 128–29.
18. Gen 18:10, 13.
19. Gen 21:1–2, 6–7.

so doing, Genesis shows they served God. They suspended adam the first rationality about their own goals. As Brueggemann says,

> Faith is not a reasonable act which fits into the normal scheme of life and perception. . . . It must come from Abraham and Sarah. "Is anything too hard for the LORD?" That is the question around which this confrontation revolves.[20]

The reader of Genesis has followed Sarah and Abraham through their journey and seen them change through their own wandering and adversities. And in this moment in chapter 18 they cease being a couple longing for land and children. They become a community of hospitality to strangers, they become faithful together in the act of trusting God enough to offer hospitality to strangers. Yes, their "adam the first" longings of land and children will be fulfilled, but their "adam the second" longing is fulfilled as well. They not only know how, but why. They have a God who knows them and loves them, and they are the beginning of the community of faith. In offering hospitality to strangers, Abraham and Sarah do not draw attention to their own glory of being made in God's image and likeness, rather, through their agency—the gift of being made in God's image and likeness—they serve others, and in so doing, they literally return glory to God.

Andrei Rublev wrote a famous icon on the subject of the hospitality of Abraham and Sarah titled "Old Testament Trinity." Rublev interpreted the three visitors as the Trinity of Christian theology, as have many others. He wrote it for the Feast of Pentecost, the coming of the Holy Spirit. Pentecost, in Eastern Orthodox thought, is the culminating action of the Holy Spirit, the fulfillment of the revelation of God as three persons. There is no specific Feast of the Trinity as in Western Christianity. Instead, Pentecost is the cause to celebrate the wholeness of the Trinity. The middle figure is the Son, who is blessing the food in the bowl. To the Son's left is the Holy Spirit, who is wearing a green robe signifying life. The Father is to the Son's right. All of the figures are seated equally

---

20. Brueggemann, *Genesis*, loc. 59.

at the table, and there is no head of the table. The faces are almost identical signifying that they are all of one being. At the same time, the faces do not obviously appear to be male or female, but they are still the faces of the three persons of the Trinity. Most significantly, Rublev has written this icon so that there is an empty place at the table, which is for those who view the icon. Rublev takes the hospitality of Abraham and Sarah and transfers it to the hospitality of the Trinity, inviting us to join them at table. In this icon the Trinity invites us, as creatures made in the image and likeness of God, to be cocreators, co-redeemers, co-sanctifiers with God, in the power of the Holy Spirit.[21] We are invited to be full participants in God.

---

21. Ouspensky and Lossky, *Meaning of Icons*, 199–202.

CHAPTER 2

Participation in God in the New Testament

THIS CHAPTER WILL MAKE the case that human longing for God is a movement within human beings by the Holy Spirit, God's own way of drawing humanity into relationship with God and rooted in God's own longing for relationship with humanity. This longing by God is made manifest in the life of Jesus, who comes seeking to draw humans into relationship with him, and is made most manifest in Jesus' practice of table fellowship. Particularly, Jesus explicates three ways of seeing the body of Christ: as his own body, in the bread of the table, and in the church, and one cannot be separated from the other.

In his letter to the Romans, Paul says,

> For all who are led by the Spirit of God are children of God. For you did not receive a spirit of slavery to fall back into fear, but you received a spirit of adoption. When we cry, "Abba! Father!" it is that very Spirit bearing witness with our spirit that we are children of God, and if children, then heirs: heirs of God and joint heirs with Christ, if we, in fact, suffer with him so that we may also be glorified with him.[1]

This passage is thought by Sarah Coakley to be the earliest reference to the three persons of God. It describes the triune God as living in human beings through the presence of the Spirit of God.

1. Rom 8:14–17.

Participation in God

The Spirit of God draws the human towards God, as God's own longing and desire for humanity, in one movement with humanity's longing for God. Coakley says of this passage,

> Vital here is Paul's analysis of prayer in Romans 8, where he describes how, strictly speaking, we do not autonomously do the praying, for we do not even really know what to ask for; rather it is the "Spirit" who prays in us to the ultimate source in God ("the Father," or "Abba") and does so with "sighs too deep for words" that tran-scend normal human rationality. Into that ceaseless divine dialogue between Spirit and "Father" the Christian prayer is thus caught up, and so transformed, becoming a co-heir with Christ and being fashioned into an extension of redeemed, incarnate life.[2]

The faith of Abraham and Sarah meant that they transcended normal human rationality when they dropped everything and provided extravagant hospitality to strangers. Led by the Spirit, they were filled with compassion and mercy for what they perceived as human beings in need, exercising their agency in compassion that was more powerful than their adam-the-first rationality, and yet they paradoxically fulfilled their adam-the-first longings. This transcended normal human rationality. In Romans, this is a sense of faith that is grounded in the death and resurrection of Jesus. It is the notion that in baptism we have died, and it is God who lives in us, through the power of the Holy Spirit. In that sense we participate in the life of God because it is the only life we have, even in our creatureliness in God's creation.

Throughout the Gospels Jesus sits at table with a wide assortment of people as he draws humanity into relationship with him, and through him to the Father and the Holy Spirit. He and his disciples eat with tax collectors and sinners. Even when at table as a guest he draws attention to those who are thought be less honorable and brings their plight into the center of the table fellowship.[3]

---

2. Coakley, *Asceticism*, loc. 1538.

3. Matt 26:6–13; Mark 14:3–9; Luke 5:27–32, 7:36–50, 11:37–54, 14:1–6, 15:1–7.

In doing so he shows that loving all people is at the heart of his teaching, regardless of cultural, social, or economic status. He challenges convention by letting himself be touched by those who are considered untouchable. As Ruth Meyers says,

> The Gospels report that Jesus ate and drank with tax collectors and sinners—such as Matthew (Matt. 9:9–13) and Zacchaeus (Luke 19:1–7)—behavior that some considered scandalous. Liturgical scholar Paul Bradshaw explains that some more pious Jews at the time of Jesus "were very careful about not only what they ate (so as to observe the dietary laws prescribed in the Old Testament) but also with whom they shared a meal, since eating with those they regarded as impure would compromise their own ritual purity." By eating both with those considered unclean and with the more pious Pharisees (Luke 7:36), Jesus embodied God's gracious and boundless love and so enacted God's mission.[4]

In the four Gospels there are six stories of Jesus feeding the multitudes, more than any other story in the Bible. When the disciples say they do not have enough to share, Jesus takes, blesses, breaks, and gives the bread. Then he gives the now multiplied bread to the disciples so that they may give it to the multitudes. At the Last Supper, before his death and resurrection, Jesus repeats the same action of taking, blessing, breaking, and giving bread, and as C. Clifton Black says, this "evoked Jesus' feeding of the multitudes."[5]

The Gospels may well be seen as a series of stories of Jesus at table. As Andrew McGowan observes,

> Although modern Christians are accustomed to understanding their own versions of this meal [the Eucharist] largely through the story of Jesus's final meal, the term "Last Supper" itself implies a whole series of previous suppers. The first Christians remembered not just the last but many meals of Jesus as models for their own eating. . . . The Gospels themselves present that final meal of

---

4. Bradshaw, *Christian Worship*, 42, quoted in Meyers, *Missional Worship*, 152.

5. Attridge and Meeks, *HarperCollins Study Bible*, 1946.

> Jesus as the climax of his practice as frequent, significant, and controversial eater.... These many not-last suppers were an important part of Jesus' ministry and contributed both to his popularity and to his conflicts; one scholar has said pointedly, "Jesus was killed because of the way he ate."... These narratives reflect the early Christians' sense of their community meals as the continuation of a whole series of Jesus' suppers or banquets, not just a memorialization of one.[6]

This quote reminds the reader that table fellowship was a central part of Jesus' ministry. Paul F. Bradshaw also says that the Last Supper is not the only supper with references to the Eucharist.

> The trend, therefore, in more recent scholarship has been to locate the source of the Eucharist more broadly within the context of other meals in Jesus' life and not merely the Last Supper, and largely following the trajectory established by redaction-criticism, to take seriously various layers of meaning that can be discerned within the New Testament and the different ways that the individual New Testament writers describe those meals.[7]

Because table fellowship was a regular part of the disciples' experience of Jesus, it draws even more attention to the uniqueness of the "last supper." That in his last meal before his crucifixion Jesus chose to say, "This is my body, this is my blood," makes that meal more exceptional among all the meals, not less. All of the meals together are remembered when the Lord's Supper is celebrated. The Christian common meal "brought into one focus a great many facets of Christian belief and expectation. It was a reminder, of course, of the Last Supper that Jesus shared with the Twelve. Beyond that, it recalled all the meals he had eaten with them in the course of his ministry. The feedings of multitudes in the wilderness were also meals of thanksgiving. At those meals too, Jesus took bread, broke it, and gave thanks."[8]

6. McGowan, *Ancient Christian Worship*, 20.
7. Bradshaw, *Eucharistic Origins*, 2.
8. Price and Weil, *Liturgy for Living*, 131.

Just as the disciples' *anamnesis* (making present by remembering) includes multiple memories and teachings, including feeding the multitudes and drawing attention to the outcast, for the church to focus on the Last Supper to the exclusion of the other meals, then, detracts from the fullness of *anamnesis* in the Lord's Supper.

The oldest written account of the Last Supper appears in Paul's first letter to the Corinthians. That the words in one of Paul's letters are so similar to those in the Synoptics, especially Luke, gives evidence that these words are part of a very early Christian tradition.[9] In his letter Paul chides those who do not share their food at the eucharistic meal with those who have little.

> For when the time comes to eat, each of you proceeds to eat your own supper, and one goes hungry and another becomes drunk. What! Do you not have households to eat and drink in? Or do you show contempt for the church of God and humiliate those who have nothing? What should I say to you? Should I commend you? In this matter I do not commend you.[10]

Paul particularly addresses the socioeconomic implications of the meal in 1 Corinthians. Paul's point is that this meal should be unlike the customary meal settings in his and many other cultures, where the affluent have the best places at the table and those who have little to nothing, most likely slaves, are in a different room with little to no food. Paul's point is that this meal is

> more than a mere "meal together"; "Surely it cannot be that you have no homes of your own for eating and drinking, can it?" (v. 22a). The present "ordering" of the so-called Lord's Supper is a travesty that puts to shame those who have nothing (v. 22b), that is, makes them experience public shame in contrast to honor.[11]

---

9. Price and Weil, *Liturgy*, 30.
10. 1 Cor 11:21–22.
11. Thiselton, *1 Corinthians*, loc. 2531.

Participation in God

The whole purpose of the letter is to address cultural, social, and economic divisions within the church in Corinth. In this meal there should be no division, and all should be equal participants in the meal, because all participate as members of Christ's body.

> In place of "This is the bread of affliction that your fathers ate ...," Jesus declared, "This is my body, which is for you" (v. 24). This "meal" was to be repeated, not to celebrate and to relive the events of the Exodus Passover, but "in remembrance of me" (v. 24b). The cup taken after supper (v. 25a) represented "the new covenant in my blood" (v. 25b). The logical force of "this is my body" is determined by the parallel "reliving" and sharing in the event in which "this is the bread of affliction ..." It is not an "is" of total identity, but denotes a "living through" that entails more than mere semantic representation. The words of the Black spiritual, "Were you 'there' when they crucified my Lord?" well conveys these dynamics of participatory involvement.... Paul brings this to an incisive focus in his own explanation of the meaning of these words and actions: For as Many times as you eat this bread and drink the cup, it is the death of the Lord that you are proclaiming, claiming, until he comes (v. 26). Each participant declares, proclaims, or preaches in the breaking of bread that "Christ died," and in eating the bread and drinking from the cup that "Christ died for me"; I appropriate his death for me; I "take" Christ as "mine," even as I take and receive broken bread and wine poured out.[12]

McGowan makes similar observations about the eucharistic meal in 1 Corinthians:

> When the table of the Lord was shared at Corinth, other questions and problems from the wider world of dining were brought along. Those who could afford to bring food were clearly eating a substantial meal (1 Cor 11:21). Paul uses the story of the Last Supper (vv. 23–25) not to give instructions for proper ritual or prayer, or to suggest consumption of mere crumbs and sips, but to shame a

---

12. Thiselton, *1 Corinthians*, loc. 2563–71.

> divided community at Corinth with the example of Jesus' humility and self-offering (vv. 27–30). We do not know what resulted in this case but should not assume that Paul's intention was to separate out a token form of eating or have such replace the communal meal. The bread and wine to be shared in his ideal banquet are still staple foods, shared fairly—not odd, merely "sacramental," additions to the meal. His advice was for moderation and above all for mutual consideration at table. Discerning the body—not only the body of Christ identified with the bread, but the body thus constituted by those who shared the bread—was the condition for celebrating a meal worthy to be thought of as "the Lord's" (1 Cor 11:27–29; cf. v. 20).[13]

In 1 Corinthians we see evidence that the eucharistic meal was a normal practice for early Christians to participate in Christ's body, and that for Paul, to be truly a way of honoring Christ's body, it required the full participation of the whole church.

Juan M. C. Oliver, former custodian of the Book of Common Prayer of the Episcopal Church, observes that,

> Eugene Laverdiere and John Koenig, among many, have studied the relationship between the kingdom and the meals recounted in the gospels. . . . They all involve recognition, usually around food, hinting perhaps to the Christian meals where we recognized the Lord in the breaking of bread. Thus, the gospels, whenever they describe Jesus and a meal, may be pointing to the eucharistic meals of the early Christians, the sign of the *basileia* (kingdom, kingship reign, royal power, rule or governance) of God in a new world transformed by truth, justice, peace, and love—the central message of Jesus.[14]

Oliver shows that the early eucharistic meals were a way to not merely experience but to live out the kingdom's presence, brought to earth by Christ, and lived out now, in the eucharistic meals of his followers.

13. McGowan, *Ancient Christian Worship*, 31.
14. Oliver, "Banquet," 27.

Participation in God

When, in 1 Corinthians and Luke, Jesus says at the Last Supper, "Do this in remembrance of me," he is not simply talking about that action at that table but alluding to his prior actions the disciples have witnessed and heard throughout Jesus' ministry. And the message is echoed in John's version of the Last Supper: "I give you a new commandment, that you love one another. Just as I have loved you, you also should love one another."[15]

> Both Scripture and the witness of the early Church point to the kingdom as God's sovereign rule over *this* world—a process of transformation already begun but reaching its fulfillment at Christ's final inspection visit, or *parousia*. . . . The eucharistic meal was thus a tangible *sign* of this expected new world: a symptom and evidence of its presence already here among us although not yet fully consummated. Two aspects gave this away: the meals were radically egalitarian and they are about love.[16]

The Eucharist was a literal feeding of body and soul, a sign and reality of the kingdom of Christ's love lived out in his body the church.

In the story of the feeding of five thousand in Matt 14, Mark 6, and Luke 9 Jesus tells his disciples, "You give them something to eat."[17] They reply that they have nothing to eat but a few loaves and fish. In Matt 15 and Mark 8 Jesus feeds four thousand from seven loaves. His actions are the same in all six stories; he takes, blesses, breaks, and gives bread enough for everyone to eat, and to have bread left over. In all six stories Jesus gives the broken bread to the disciples to distribute to the crowd, and the disciples give everyone something to eat.

After his resurrection Jesus resumes his table practice. In Luke 24 the disciples encounter Jesus as they are walking to Emmaus, but they do not recognize Jesus. As they tell this apparent stranger of the tragic and bewildering events of Jesus' death and appearance afterwards to some disciples, they still do not recognize him. But

---

15. John 13:34.
16. Oliver, "Banquet," 26.
17. Matt 14:16, Mark 6:37, Luke 9:13.

as they approach Emmaus in the evening, they offer this stranger the hospitality of a meal and a place to stay.

> When he was at the table with them, he took bread, blessed and broke it, and gave it to them. Then their eyes were opened, and they recognized him, and he vanished from their sight. They said to each other, "Were not our hearts burning within us while he was talking to us on the road, while he was opening the scriptures to us?" That same hour they got up and returned to Jerusalem, and they found the eleven and their companions gathered together. They were saying, "The Lord has risen indeed, and he has appeared to Simon!" Then they told what had happened on the road and how he had been made known to them in the breaking of the bread.[18]

In this moment in Luke the disciples recognize Jesus when he takes, blesses, breaks, and gives bread. In the Last Supper of Luke, after Jesus had taken, blessed, broken, and given bread, he said, "Do this in remembrance of me" (22:19). Here he verifies what he has commanded.

In John 21 Jesus prepares breakfast for the disciples on the beach while they are fishing but having no success. They did not recognize Jesus until he told them to cast their nets on the opposite side of the boat, and when their nets were too full to haul them into the boat, they recognized Jesus.

When the disciples returned to the beach they found Jesus grilling bread and fish, the same food from the feeding of the multitude, and he gave it to them to eat. It is in this context, after Jesus has provided a breakfast of bread and fish, that he has a conversation with Peter. Three times Jesus asks Peter if he loves him. Each time Peter says that he loves Jesus. In response to Peter Jesus says, "Feed my lambs. . . . Tend my sheep. . . . Feed my sheep" (vv. 15-17). Here, Jesus gives Peter his final commission in the Gospel of John. When Jesus first called Peter, he was a fisherman. Now Jesus has been crucified and risen, but Peter has simply returned to fishing. Jesus, having once again multiplied fish, tells Peter to feed

---

18. Luke 24:30-35.

Jesus' sheep. Peter is still a fisherman but a fisherman who serves the shepherd's sheep. Peter is at once called to gather and to feed those he gathers. The sheep belong to Jesus, not Peter, and Peter serves Jesus by feeding his sheep. The question may arise, Who are the lambs and sheep Peter is supposed to feed and tend? For generations commentators and theologians have said the answer is the church. But who is the church? The answer appears in six stories (and in Paul's first letter to the Corinthians). Adele Reinhartz sees the loaves and fishes on the fire as a specific recollection of the multiplication of loaves and fishes in feeding the multitude in John 6.[19] Peter, and those who follow Jesus, are to take, bless, break, and give their lives for the hungry multitudes.

As did Abraham and Sarah, Jesus exercises radical hospitality to all types and conditions of people throughout his life and ministry. While he does so, he also instructs his disciples to do the same—in his instructions at the feeding of the multitude "you give them something to eat," in his new commandment to the disciples at the Last Supper in John to "love one another as I love you," and in his commandment to Peter in John to "feed my sheep." As did Abraham and Sarah, Jesus shows that we fulfill our humanity when we use our power to serve those in need.

In several places in the New Testament the motif of meal and banquet is mentioned in reference to heaven, and these references are related to meals on earth. Matthew 25:31–46 captures and reframes the message of Gen 18. Jesus tells a story about the parousia, and the King in the story is the Son of Man. As with Abraham and Sarah feeding the divine while being unaware of who they were serving, in this story those who feed the hungry, give the thirsty something to drink, welcome the stranger, clothe the naked, take care of the sick, and visit those in prison are serving the King, the Son of Man. "Truly I tell you, just as you did it to one of the least of these brothers and sisters of mine, you did it to me." Because they did so they are heirs of the kingdom. But those who fail to do so "will go away into eternal punishment."[20]

19. Reinhartz, *John*, 196.
20. Matt 25:40, 46.

Participation in God in the New Testament

The New Testament shows that when the church as the body of Christ serves, we participate in the life of God by serving as Christ has served us. Not only are we no longer alone and estranged from one another, but we are one with ourselves because we are fulfilling our humanity. The New Testament shows that we participate in God's life not merely by sitting at table and receiving but by bringing all to the table and giving to all. When we gather at table, feeding all so that no one is hungry, we are the adam God created us to be, by being joined into the body of the new Adam. When we feed the hungry, give drink to the thirsty, welcome the stranger, clothe the naked, take care of the sick, and visit those in prison, we participate in the life of God. We participate in God's life when we serve one another as Christ served us. We participate in the life of God when we transcend normal rationality and embrace the other.

CHAPTER 3

Coming to Faith and Praising God

IN LIGHT OF THE COVID-19 pandemic, I explore the work of various theologians to provide a theology of worship that is rooted in Christianity but is not dependent on sacramental practice, or even in-person worship, while also pointing to the sacraments and participation in them as participating in God. Specifically, I will focus on home table prayers and meals in Jewish heritage and eucharistic history and on current practice, especially in the post-COVID era.

As Soloveitchik has described, there is a basic human perspective of being a creature on earth, as one kind of creature among many. Yet, there is also a human awareness that human creatureliness is unique among the creatures. This distinctiveness among the creatures may lead to two divergent attitudes. The attitude of adam the first is domination, exercising dominion of creation as the dominant force in creation, making creation subject to human will and desire. The second attitude, the attitude of adam the second, is stewardship of creation and the other creatures of earth. Both domination and stewardship acknowledge the uniqueness of humanity and the power humans have in creation. What sets these two views apart is how they view their relationship not merely with creation but with the Creator, God.

Adam the first sees creation as existing to serve humanity, to fulfill human needs and wants. To the degree that adam the first is concerned about the sustainability of creation, this concern arises when the possibility appears that creation may fail to provide what humans need and want. Adam the second sees creation as a gift from God, the ecology of the very gift of life itself. Perceiving that creation belongs to God, humanity's role in creation is to exercise stewardship of creation as part of humanity's role in serving God. From the perspective of adam the second, the fact that creation fulfills human needs and wants is a blessing of God's creation, rather than the goal, and is a sign of God's love to humanity.

Berakah prayers, ancient Jewish prayers said over meals, have the words, "Blessed are you, Lord our God, Ruler of the universe, who brings forth bread from the earth," and "Blessed are you, O Lord our God, Ruler of the universe, who creates the fruit of the vine."[1] These prayers proclaim that God is ruler of the universe and that, with God providing humans the skill and energy required to produce bread and wine, it is God who brings forth bread and wine from the earth. The prayer depicts the human as servant—first, a servant to God and, second, a servant specifically within God's creation. The very act of producing bread to satisfy hunger is God's own loving action within humanity. To proclaim God as ruler of the universe is to praise God, and to give thanks for life itself, seen as a gift from God. A prayer of blessing is a prayer of thanksgiving for what God has provided in producing fruit of the earth and that thanks God for providing adam with skill and energy to produce bread and wine from the fruit of the earth. Blessing acknowledges the skill and dignity of adam the first who takes natural agricultural products and transforms them into food and wine, prayed from the perspective of adam the second, by not claiming all the glory but by acknowledging that it is God who has provided all, returning the glory to God.

Significantly, berakah prayers are said at home over the Friday evening sabbath meal. The prayers are not specifically for what is commonly considered public or corporate worship, but they are prayers for meals at home.[2] On the subject of blessing, Andrew Davison says,

1. "Blessings," paras. 3–4.
2. "Blessings," para. 1.

Participation in God

> A good place to start is with blessing as thankful recognition, not least in the most common of "blessings": what we call grace or the blessing of a meal. This theme also suggests that any services or occasions for blessing should contain some explicit mention that God is creator and some explicit recognition that what we bless has come from him.... Blessing, then, takes in speaking well of God as well as speaking well of his creation. That, in turn, has suggested a second element that should also be present in every act of blessing, namely some element of praise. We see that in words that open a common form of prayer of blessing: "Blessed art thou, Lord God of all creation." Just as a blessing properly includes recognition of God as creator, it should also ascribe praise to God and recognize his holiness.[3]

This places the practice and attitudes of blessing and praise in the household, and specifically at the table. Yet, McGowan observes, "meals described in the Dead Sea Scrolls, which are as old as the Gospels or older, as well as in the later Mishnah, involve blessings for an opening cup with a characteristic prayer of *berakah* ('blessing') form: 'Blessed are you Lord God, King of the universe,' followed by a specific petition."[4] This is an early indicator that what became public prayers have their origin in blessings over the meal in households.

Daniel Hardy and David Ford observe that Jesus would have used such prayers of blessing.

> Blessing is the comprehensive praise and thanks that returns all reality to God, and so lets all be taken up into the spiral of mutual appreciation and delight which is the fulfilment of creation. For the rabbis of Jesus' time, to use anything of creation without blessing God was to rob God. Only the person receiving with thanks really received from God, and if there is one summary expression of Jewish response to God it is in the blessing of his name, which represents his whole being. Jesus was in

---

3. Davison, *Blessing*, loc. 123, 141.
4. McGowan, *Ancient Christian Worship*, 25.

this tradition, and himself blessed God, food, children and disciples. His whole work is summed up in Acts as having been sent to bless, completing the history of the blessing of Israel through Abraham (Acts 3:25f). Jesus is seen as the concentration of the mutuality of blessing, God blessing [adam] and [adam] blessing God. This is the dynamic of both creation and reconciliation.[5]

Praise of God is not a separate form of prayer but is inherent in the very notion of blessing. Creation as such is a blessing, and creation itself praises God.

> Praise is therefore best seen as part of an ecology of blessing. All creation is a part of this, and praises God. What meaning can be given to this? Two levels appear in it. The first is that, since God's blessing is given by letting each creature, animate or not, be itself, and by enabling it, with infinite respect for its nature, to participate in the drama of the universe, then creation's response is primarily in its very existence. Creation's praise is not an extra, an addition to what it is, but is the shining of its being, the overflowing significance it has in pointing to its Creator simply by being itself.
>
> The second level is the way this being can overflow into many forms of expression. When the glory of creation is glimpsed it can inspire painting, psalms, music, science, literature and a vast variety of less formal recognition and appreciation. This is the role of human beings in creation, articulating its praise in fresh ways.[6]

Therefore, in the berakah God is first praised as Creator, and then thanks are offered for food and wine, the life sustaining produce of creation. However, McGowan cautions against drawing too straight a line between what became the "seder as depicted in the Mishnah" and the Last Supper, or any Jewish meals in the time of Jesus, since the seder "may not have been fully developed, let alone universally observed, at the time of Jesus; the later rabbinic form may even owe something to the Christian eucharistic tradition and

---

5. Hardy and Ford, *Jubilate*, 81–82.
6. Hardy and Ford, *Jubilate*, 82.

Participation in God

reflect responses to it. If the Last Supper was a Passover banquet as seems likely, it is nevertheless misleading to see the Eucharist as a sort of Christianized seder in that later and more developed sense."[7]

Still, it seems quite likely that Jewish custom in the time of Jesus was to pray the berakah and that some form of the prayer existed centuries before Jesus. On this point, Robert Verrill says,

> Such prayers of blessing occur throughout the bible: "*Blessed is the Lord for ever*" (Ps. 89.52), "*Blessed be the Lord who has given his people Israel rest as he promised: not one of the promises he made through his servant Moses has failed*" (1 Kings 8:56), "*Blessed be God's name from age to age for all wisdom and power are his*" (Dan 2:20). Often such blessings occur with other elements such as a supplication or a thanksgiving (hodayah). For instance, Solomon's berakah above continues with a supplication: "*The Lord our God be with us as he was with our forefathers; may he never leave us nor forsake us*" (1 Kings 8:57). Daniel's berakah continues with an expression of thanks: "*To thee, God of my fathers, I give thanks and praise, for thou hast given me wisdom and power*" (Dan 2:23). And of course, Jesus is recorded as saying the blessing and giving thanks during the Last Supper.
>
> It is likely that in the 1st Century AD, it would have been very typical for Jews to say a grace at the end of meals that contained a berakah together with a hodayah (a thanksgiving) and a supplication. Praising God is a blessing for those who bless him. The Jews blessed and thanked God for his past actions such as their liberation from Egyptian slavery, but they also looked to the future.[8]

Barry Hudock affirms the Jewish tradition of Jesus' prayers.

> The eucharistic prayer is rooted in the prayer Jesus prayed at the Last Supper. But Jesus was not simply ad-libbing a new and original prayer that evening. He was a faithful

---

7. McGowan, *Ancient Christian Worship*, 24–25.
8. Verrill, "A–Z of the Mass," paras. 1–2 (italics original).

> Jewish man, and one aspect of the life of every faithful Jew was the prayer known as the *berakah*. Because of the *berakah's* place in the history and development of the Eucharist, Louis Bouyer called it "providence's preparatory work." In the New Testament, Jesus prays it often (Matt 11:25; Luke 10:21; John 11:41–43). The thanksgivings with which Paul opens almost every one of his letters reflect his and his audience's familiarity with the *berakah*. . . . With this background it becomes clear that when we read that Jesus at the Last Supper "said the blessing" over bread and "gave thanks" over a cup (Matt 26:26, 27), these are references to *berakoth*. The evangelists don't ever bother to provide the actual words, because they were very familiar to their readers. The only words the evangelists do record are the ones that were novel, the places where what Jesus said represented a startling and unexpected deviation from what the disciples would have expected.[9]

This focus on blessing with thanksgiving is older than Christian congregational worship, and yet Christian congregational worship is shaped by blessing. That an individual would willingly seek out and participate in congregational worship attests to a desire to offer blessing, to acknowledge one's own need for God, and along with the need for God, to join with others in praising God.

In the era of quarantine and lock down, congregations discovered new ways to gather virtually. While not gathered around a table per se, people still gathered in worship and prayer. Even if not strictly using the form of the berakah, the compulsion to gather specifically in prayer, rather than the myriad other reasons people gather virtually, was and is motivated by the notion that God is God of creation and therefore of all of us, and God is the source of our coming together in whatever media humans may use because God is the Creator of all of us. This sense of the "us-ness" of humanity, and humanity with God, is at the heart of berakah, and at the heart of human longing for community.

---

9. Hudock, *Eucharistic Prayer*, 39–40.

Participation in God

A fascinating illustration of this point is made in the film *Don't Look Up*. Ostensibly, the film is about a comet that is on a collision path with the earth, the two scientists who discover this fact, and their great difficulty in getting government officials and the public to accept that the destruction of the earth will occur in six months. Obliquely, the comet is a metaphor for global warming. The film satirizes any number of current aspects of contemporary culture.

In the final scene before the credits (within which there are two additional scenes), as the collision with the comet is imminent, one of the scientists prepares a meal at home with family and friends. These are the people who have known more than anyone else in the movie what is going to happen. Their final act is to go grocery shopping, prepare a meal together, and sit at table together eating food and drinking wine, an ultimate "last supper." Before they eat, they take turns giving thanks—a sort of Eucharist, as it were. Then one of the scientists, who acknowledges his lack of a "religious" orientation, suggests that they should have some sort of concluding prayer, perhaps simply by saying amen.

The boyfriend of one of the scientists, named Yule, was raised by parents who are evangelical Christians, some of whose tenets he has rejected, such as suspicion of science, yet he has forged his own relationship with God. Beckoned by the scientists, it is Yule who prays aloud. He stretches out his hands to the people next to him, and everyone takes the hand of the person they are sitting next to. He prays, "Dearest Father and Almighty Creator, we ask for your grace tonight despite our pride, your forgiveness despite our doubt. Most of all Lord we ask for your love, to soothe us through these dark times. May we face whatever is to come in your divine will with courage and open hearts of acceptance. Amen." And one of the scientists responds, "Wow, you have got some church game!" As the meal proceeds the conversation turns to food—whether people prefer real mashed potatoes to instant and why and whether it is worth the effort to grind one's own coffee beans. The lead scientist says, "We really did have everything, didn't we? I mean, when you think about it." And then the comet hits.

Coming to Faith and Praising God

After the earth is destroyed, various items are seen floating through space. The first identifiable item is a cell phone, whose screen says, "Congratulations! You hit your diet goal," followed by a luxury car, and then the bronze bull statue from Wall Street. In the next scene, which occurs well into the credits, the president of the United States and a billionaire who builds his own space crafts have escaped earth to be cryogenically preserved with other billionaires on another planet. Upon landing on another planet thousands of years later, they are immediately eaten by animals native to that planet. But the president forgets to take her chief of staff with her, who also happens to be her son. In a post-credit scene, he emerges from a destroyed building, and all around him is destruction. After crying for his mom, he pulls out his mobile phone to make a social-media post and says, "What's up, y'all? I'm the last man on Earth," and signs off with, "Don't forget to like and subscribe."[10]

Numerous commentators have highlighted the dinner scene in their reviews of the film. Yule is played by Timothée Chalamet. When director Adam McKay first approached Chalamet about playing the role of Yule, Chalamet's first response was, "Yeah, I don't know if there's enough there," and McKay agreed. Then McKay was talking this over with coproducer Ron Suskind who asked, "Where's faith in this movie?" to which McKay responded, "Oh, you're right. You're right!" McKay explained, "I think we're so used to thinking of religion as denominations, and now it's become a political cudgel in this country. I forgot about real faith. And it was just a lightbulb moment where it's like, 'I know who Timothée's character is.'" McKay, whose mother was a born-again Christian, said it was that scene that hooked Chalamet. With the addition of Chalamet's Yule, McKay said, "the team was complete," adding, "And that might be my single favorite moment in the entire movie."[11]

Don't Look Up provides vivid examples of Soloveitchik's two adams, even if the examples are slightly absurd. What is most

10. McKay, *Don't Look Up*.
11. Arthur, "On the Ending(s)," paras. 16–18.

interesting is the transformation of the two scientists, the prophets of the destruction of the earth. They move from adam the first rationality, trying to convince everyone they are right, to the ones who are the humblest, the most like adam the second. At the opposite end are those who are most like adam the first, who believe that they have the rational means to destroy the comet and, if not destroy it, then to escape its consequences while leaving the rest of humanity to die. With the destruction of earth an imminent certainty, "adam the second" humbly gathers at table, gives thanks for all of life, and prays to God for grace, forgiveness, and love.

Adam the first believes that food is a right. Adam the second sees food only as the result of toil and sweat. Both are correct, and both are wrong. Adam the first does have a right to food, but so does every adam. Adam the second is correct in that food is the result of sweat and toil. Yet that sweat and toil, or earning the means to purchase the result of the sweat and toil of others, is part of the privilege of being a human. Adam the first has skill, ingenuity, and energy to produce food, all of which are gifts of God-given human life. And adam the second sees that using those gifts costs sweat and toil, either by one's own efforts, or the efforts of others. What both adams are lacking on their own is gratitude, thanksgiving, eucharist, berakah—blessing God. When God is blessed for the gift of food then both adams see that life-sustaining food is the most essential gift and sign of God's love, other than life itself, and that sharing food with people who are hungry is in fact sharing love and life. To share food is to reflect God, to participate in the abundant life-giving power of the Trinity. When people are starving, food offered to them is not mere hospitality, as in showing a good time or throwing a party. Giving food to starving people is giving life and sharing God's most essential sign of God's love for all adams, and it is participating in God's life of offering and giving life to others. And yet, *giving* food is simpler than and less socially challenging than *sharing* food. Giving food keeps the relationship one way, from giver to receiver. Sitting at table together and sharing food levels the social relationship, it crosses the chasms of social structures.

In the story of the rich man and Lazarus in Luke 16:19–31, Lazarus was a poor man who longed to satisfy his hunger from what fell from the rich man's table, without satisfaction. Lazarus has died and has been carried away by angels to be with Abraham. The rich man also died and went to Hades where he saw Abraham far away with Lazarus at his side. It is now the rich man who wants Lazarus to comfort him by dipping his finger in water and cooling the rich man's tongue. Yet Abraham responds, "Child, remember that during your lifetime you received your good things, and Lazarus in like manner evil things; but now he is comforted here, and you are in agony. Besides all this, between you and us a great chasm has been fixed, so that those who might want to pass from here to you cannot do so, and no one can cross from here to us."

The rich man has no gratitude, no berakah, no eucharist. If the rich man had simply given Lazarus enough to sustain him that would have been loving, sharing God's gift of food enough to sustain someone else's life. But if the rich man had invited Lazarus to sit at table with him, to dine with him, that would have been the beginning of relationship, of breaking bread together, of not just crossing the chasm, but closing the chasm bit by bit.

In Luke 14:7–14 Jesus makes the point that conventional socially stratified relationships have no place in the kingdom of God. If one is a guest at a banquet, one should always enter humbly. If one gives a banquet, one should invite "the poor, the crippled, the lame, and the blind. And you will be blessed, because they cannot repay you, for you will be repaid at the resurrection of the righteous."[12]

In a time of social isolation, when berakah may by necessity be prayed alone, focusing on the "us-ness" of creaturehood and creation means that when we partake of food, we all partake from the same one earth, whether alone or with others. We partake of the one creation and are joined in our mutual partaking. We partake of one another as creatures whose bodies return to the earth, dust to dust, becoming earth again, producing food for later generations. Some of that food becomes bread and wine, set aside,

---

12. Luke 14:13–14.

consecrated, as Christ's own body and blood, reminding us that what came into being at the beginning came into being through him and is his own life. Our human bodies are entwined with each other, and entwined with God's creation, and thus with God, Father, Son, and Holy Spirit.

Every meal is a partaking of God's one creation, and of God's own life given for us in creation. Christ makes real and incarnate that which has always been true for human life. When we eat, whether alone or with others, we participate in God's own life, and we participate with one another's lives. Indeed, "Blessed are you O Lord, *our* God, for you give *us* food and drink from the earth to sustain *our* lives, and to make *our* hearts glad."[13] Whenever any of us eats—whether in a huge banquet, alone in an apartment, sitting under the stars in the desert, or at home with our families—all are social occasions. And thus, all are moments of participation in God. Jesus did not teach us to pray, "My father, give me today my daily bread" but "*Our* Father . . . give *us* today *our* daily bread."[14]

---

13. *Book of Common Prayer*, 835 (italics added).
14. Matt 6:9, 11 (italics added).

CHAPTER 4

Baptism and Eucharist

IN THIS CHAPTER I will examine the roles of holy baptism and the Eucharist in the practice of the Episcopal Church as ways people participate in the priesthood of Christ, fulfilling their ministries as participants in the worship, mission, and governance of the church. Restoring the full eucharistic meal will be considered as a means of fully participating in the body of Christ. I will make the argument that fulfilling the promises of the baptismal covenant is the challenge of Christians throughout their lives. And I will show how the historic Jewish and Christian actions of taking, blessing, breaking, and giving point to a pattern of transformation, from one degree of glory to another.

In previous chapters I have written about participation in God based on human longing for God and for community, and the notion of the "two adams" as two ways humans may approach their relationship with God, with creation, and with each other. In the immediately preceding chapter, I focused on the notion of blessing, based on the Jewish berakah prayer, as a means and example of participating in God and communal life any time food is eaten. This basis of participating in God through a household meal is now brought into understanding the church.

At first, it may seem that what is generally regarded as a two-thousand-year-old institution with myriad iterations, theologies, canons, rules, structures, and varying degrees of influence in historic and current social life has little to do with common, household life. Yet, the very word "church" comes from the Greek word *kuriakon—kuria* or "lord," plus *oikos* or "house," meaning "the Lord's house." The more commonly used word in the Greek New Testament that is translated into the English word "church" is *ecclesia—ecto* or "called" plus *kalein* or "out," meaning "called out"—and was originally used to describe an assembly of citizens in the ancient Greek state. The Greek root word, *oikos*, is also in some other significant words. The word parish, from *para-oikos*, means near house. Diocese, from *dia-oikein*, means across houses. Ecumenical, from *oiko-umene*, means whole house. Ecology comes from *oiko-logia*, house talk. And economy, from *oikos-nemein*, means house management.[1] I raise this point here to draw attention to the loss of the notion of household in how the above words are currently used. In particular, I draw attention to the notion of the church as God's household.

When the word church is translated from either *kuriakon* or *ecclesia* in the New Testament, it is never in reference to a building but a people. When one joins the church, one is joining a household, the head of which is God. One is not born into this household, even if one is born into a Christian family. Rather, one is reborn by adoption and grace into the household of God, the church, by holy baptism. In the baptismal rite of the Episcopal Church, when the congregation welcomes the newly baptized, they say, "We receive you into the household of God. Confess the faith of Christ crucified, proclaim his resurrection, and share with us in his eternal priesthood."[2]

The word "we" in this welcome is not merely the "we" of the congregation present in the near household of God. It is the "we" of the whole household of God, the *oiko-umene*, which includes not only the church on earth, but the whole communion of saints in heaven as well. By virtue of holy baptism, one is admitted to the household meal, the Eucharist, not only as a recipient of Christ's

---

1. *American Heritage Dictionary*, s.vv. "church," "parish," "diocese," "ecumenical," "ecology," "economy."

2. *Book of Common Prayer*, 308.

body and blood in the bread and wine from the table but as an active participant in the priesthood of Christ, a co-consecrator by the power of the Holy Spirit of the meal, with other members of the household in a near house (*para-oikos*), across the numerous households of a diocese (*dia-oikein*), over which an elder presides on behalf of the whole household (*oiko-umene*). By entering the communion of saints in baptism one is then able to co-make Eucharist "with Angels and Archangels and with all the company of heaven."[3]

It is well documented that, in the early days of Christianity, the Eucharist was a full meal, as in a household, with special prayers said for bread and wine to be Christ's body and blood.[4] Over time, the practice of having a meal with the Eucharist was dropped. While every Eucharist with bread and wine is valid sacramentally, when there is no meal with the Eucharist we lose the sense that originally the Eucharist was a meal that satisfied physical and spiritual hunger. And we lose the communal bonding that happens in a meal.

Oliver maintains that when the meal was dropped, a trajectory began that led to the "dematerialization" of the Eucharist and the gradual weakening of its "eschatological dimension as the messianic banquet of the kingdom, sending it all farther and farther away, all the way to heaven."

> The eucharist went from a full meal in service to God and the poor, sign and foretaste of the new society, to a token meal of bread and wine *performed for* worshippers on the *way* to the kingdom, and later, to an entirely dematerialized optical event in the individual's consciousness. Our physical gathering went from being *essential* to the eschatological meaning of the eucharist to being a promise of a disembodied eternal life in a hereafter.[5]

---

3. *Book of Common Prayer*, 361.

4. 1 Cor 11:17–26; Bradshaw, *Christian Worship*, 13–14; Price and Weil, *Liturgy for Living*, 131; McGowan, *Ancient Christian Worship*; Hatchett, *American Prayer Book*, 291.

5. Oliver, "Banquet," 29 (italics original).

The eucharistic community is constituted by holy baptism. In the third chapter of Galatians Paul refers to the faith of Abraham to illustrate the important distinction between baptismal faith and following the law.

Shaye J. D. Cohen provides examples that help illuminate Paul's argument: "The law in general, and circumcision in particular, maintain social distinctions."[6] She points out that according to the Talmudic tractate Berakot, Judah says that a man is obligated daily to recite, "Blessed is God who has not made me a Gentile, who has not made me a boor, who has not made me a woman."[7] These three still appear in the Orthodox Jewish prayer book. Some versions substitute the word slave for boor.[8] Paul makes the case that baptismal faith changes this.

> But now that faith has come, we are no longer subject to a disciplinarian, for in Christ Jesus you are all children of God through faith. As many of you as were baptized into Christ have clothed yourselves with Christ. There is no longer Jew or Greek, there is no longer slave or free; there is no longer male or female, for all of you are one in Christ Jesus.[9]

Paul is here not only describing a baptismal theology, but a baptismal community that gathers at a eucharistic meal without distinctions, where all sit down at the same table without regard to earthly social, economic, racial, or political distinctions since all are now clothed with Christ, members of the same household of God, participants in the kingdom of God, and sharing in the priesthood of Christ.

Oliver makes the claim that in early days the Eucharist was experienced as an eschatological enactment of the kingdom of God, the heavenly Jerusalem, come down to earth and evolved in a gradual abridgement until the kingdom "went off to heaven." This had the consequence of changing the eschatological dimension of

---

6. Cohen, *Galatians*, 339.
7. Tosefta Berakot 6:18.
8. Cohen, *Galatians*, 339.
9. Gal 3:25–28.

the Eucharist to something only in the future, not Jesus' reign on earth now. For Oliver, this led to the consequence of promoting an individualistic, clericalist, and consumerist spirituality, and a focus on receiving communion as a private affair, disconnected from physical life and community.[10]

Also what is lost without the meal is much that is implied in the berakah: the relationship between God, creation, and us, giving thanks as the household of God for the produce and fruit of the earth, most especially the bread and wine as Christ's body and blood, but also the food of our bodily sustenance. Over time, the church minimized the berakah that Jesus and early Christians would have used and only the modified words from the Last Supper in the Synoptic Gospels and Paul's letters were used in the Eucharist. "The rituals before the meal (the taking of bread, blessing God over it, breaking the bread, and sharing it) and the rituals following it (taking the cup, blessing God over it, and sharing the wine) were compressed into a rite which consisted of taking the bread and wine together and blessing God over them, then breaking and distributing the bread and sharing the cup. The meal, separated from these significant actions, in some places developed into an agape."[11] What was a meal with rituals became rituals without a meal.

The original connection between berakah, the meal, community, and the Eucharist has become invisible but not lost. As Mark Drew says,

> The phenomenon of blessing is well known to anthropologists and sociologists of religion. Its long history predates the emergence of Judeo-Christian revealed religion by many millennia.... These are the daily prayers of praise which Christ himself would have known and used, accompanying every meaningful gesture of daily life, and most significantly meals, when God is acknowledged as source of life and sustenance. The Paschal meal was of course the most notable of these "blessings," where the thanksgiving is directed to the God who saved his people

---

10. Oliver, "Banquet," 36.
11. Hatchett, *American Prayer Book*, 291.

> from slavery in Egypt, and our Lord himself gave a new meaning to these rites when, having said the berakoth over the bread and the cup, he gave to the Church his people the saving mysteries of his body and blood, thus uniting in a single act the "upward" and "downward" meanings of the verb. The Eucharist is thus the supreme "blessing": the perfect sacrifice of praise to the Father, and the transmission in return of his most perfect gift to his Church, that of his only Son.[12]

Without a meal, the very context of berakah and the berakah in the Last Supper become invisible. Note, I am not questioning the sacramental validity of a Eucharist without a meal. I am making the case that a piece of bread and a sip of wine does not a supper make. All who receive the sacrament of bread and wine receive the fullness of the "inward and spiritual grace," but without a meal they do not see or experience the fullness of the "outward and visible sign."[13]

In the section "Concerning the Service," prior to the baptismal rite of the Book of Common Prayer 1979 of the Episcopal Church, the first sentence reads, "Holy Baptism is full initiation by water and the Holy Spirit into Christ's Body, the church. The bond which God establishes in Baptism is indissoluble."[14] In baptism, one puts on the new Adam, Jesus Christ, who by his incarnation and ministry restores, reconciles, and fulfills both adam the first and adam the second. All the dignity, knowledge, power, and glory of adam the first is restored in Christ. And yet it is also laid down by Christ as he becomes the perfect adam the second, using all his agency for redemption, compassion, and love.

Christ answers the two questions asked by the two adams by perfectly fulfilling and reconciling both adams. As put forth earlier, adam the first asks adam the second, What is the good of having compassion and love without power to accomplish them? And adam the second asks adam the first, What is the good of having power if it is not used for compassion and love? The dialogical

12. Drew, introduction to *Consecrations*, 1.
13. *Book of Common Prayer*, 857.
14. *Book of Common Prayer*, 298.

dance of the two adams leads to glorification, not glorification of adam but glorification of God, from one degree of glory to another. Jesus Christ perfectly answers both questions in perfectly being who he is called to be, and in so doing becomes the new Adam.

As Paul's letter to the church in Philippi says,

> Let the same mind be in you that was in Christ Jesus,
>
> > who, though he existed in the form of God,
> > > did not regard equality with God
> > > as something to be grasped,
> > but emptied himself,
> > > taking the form of a slave,
> > > assuming human likeness.
> > And being found in apperance as a human,
> > > he humbled himself
> > > and became obedient to the point of death—
> > > even death on a cross.
>
> > Therefore God exalted him even more highly
> > > and gave him the name
> > > that is above every other name,
> > so that at the name given to Jesus
> > > every knee should bend,
> > > in heaven and on earth and under the earth,
> > and every tongue should confess
> > > that Jesus Christ is Lord,
> > > to the glory of God the Father.[15]

This hymn, which was inserted by Paul into the letter, probably comes from an early baptismal liturgy. As Michael Cook observes,

> This early Christological hymn portrays the preexistent Christ as graciously laying aside his extraordinary position of equality with God, emptying himself by incarnation—taking on the form of a servant. . . . If the one in the "form of God" could humbly abdicate the dignity of his original status so as to suffer in order to show love for humankind, can the Philippians refrain from following his conduct?[16]

15. Phil 2:5–11.
16. Cook, *Philippians*, 357.

This sense of obedience to the point of death is in the baptismal liturgy in the Book of Common Prayer. The first reference comes at the concluding prayer to the baptismal covenant, "Grant, O Lord, that all who are baptized into the death of Jesus Christ your Son may live in the power of his resurrection and look for him to come again in glory; who lives and reigns now and forever." It comes up again in the thanksgiving over the water, "We thank you, Father, for the water of baptism. In it we are buried with Christ in his death. By it we share in his resurrection. Through it we are reborn by the Holy Spirit."[17] In the framework of Soloveitchik's two adams, they each die in holy baptism, and the newly baptized put on the new Adam by the power of the Holy Spirit.

The baptismal covenant provides challenges to anyone who strives to fulfill the vows of baptism. To truly fulfill them it takes incarnating the new Adam, Jesus Christ. As Christ fulfilled both adams, "wise as a serpent" (adam the first) and "innocent as a dove" (adam the second),[18] we need both adams to fulfill the new Adam in us. Just as Jesus Christ fulfilled his mission in his life, through his ministry, death, and resurrection, our mission is fulfilled when we fulfill Christ's priesthood through the baptismal covenant. Together with Christ, the household of God has a mission.

In the Book of Common Prayer, a section titled "An Outline of the Faith: Commonly called the Catechism" reads,

> Q. What is the mission of the Church?
>
> A. The mission of the Church is to restore all people to unity with God and each other in Christ.
>
> Q. How does the Church pursue its mission?
>
> A. The Church pursues its mission as it prays and worships, proclaims the Gospel, and promotes justice, peace, and love.
>
> Q. Through whom does the Church carry out its mission?
>
> A. The Church carries out its mission through the ministry of all its members.

17. *Book of Common Prayer*, 306.
18. Matt 10:16.

Baptism and Eucharist

Q. Who are the ministers of the Church?

A. The minister of the Church are lay persons, bishops, priests, and deacons.

Q. What is the ministry of the laity?

A. The ministry of lay persons is to represent Christ and his Church: to bear witness to him wherever they may be; and, according to the gifts given them, to carry on Christ's work of reconciliation in the world; and to take their place in the life, worship, and governance of the Church.[19]

Prior to all of this, in a general section entitled "Concerning the Service of the Church," one reads,

> The Holy Eucharist, the principal act of Christian worship on the Lord's Day and other major Feasts, and Daily Morning and Evening Prayer, as set forth in this Book, are the regular services appointed for public worship in the Church. . . . In all services, the entire Christian assembly participates in such a way that the members of each order within the Church, lay persons, bishops, priests, and deacons, fulfill the functions proper to their respective orders, as set forth in the rubrical directions for each service.[20]

The explicit language regarding baptism as "full initiation by the water and the Holy Spirit into Christ's Body, the Church," is a change from prior prayer books of the Episcopal Church as well as the Church of England. Similarly, the 1979 Book of Common Prayer is the first prayer book in the Episcopal Church to clearly state that the Eucharist is the principal act of worship on Sunday and other major feasts.

The 1979 Book of Common Prayer was the first authorized Book of Common Prayer in Anglicanism to include the proper liturgies for special days and liturgies for Ash Wednesday, Palm Sunday, Maundy Thursday, Good Friday, Holy Saturday, and the great vigil of Easter. In this book holy baptism is intentionally connected

---

19. *Book of Common Prayer*, 855.
20. *Book of Common Prayer*, 13.

with the death and resurrection of Jesus Christ by making it, or the renewal of baptismal vows, a required part of the great vigil of Easter, clearly connecting Christ's death and resurrection to our death and resurrection in Christ through holy baptism. Further, the prayer book designates other days specifically connected to the priesthood of Jesus as appropriate days for baptism and recommends reserving baptism for those days, including "the Easter Vigil, which signifies baptism as death and resurrection—the Pauline emphasis; the Day of Pentecost, which signifies baptism as the receiving of the Holy Spirit—the Lukan emphasis; the first Sunday after the Epiphany: The baptism of our Lord, which signifies baptism as new birth, regeneration—the Johannine emphasis; All Saints' Day or the Sunday after All Saints' Day, which signifies baptism as the reception into the communion of saints; and the time of the visitation of the bishop, which signifies baptism as the reception into the holy catholic church."[21] In all these ways the 1979 Book of Common Prayer of the Episcopal Church makes holy baptism the foundation of life, worship, and governance of the church.

Now in the Episcopal Church baptism is understood as full initiation into Christ's body the church. Prior to the 1979 prayer book, one had to be confirmed by a bishop before being allowed to receive Holy Communion. With this prayer book, all who are baptized are admitted to Holy Communion, whether children who have not yet been confirmed or adults who were baptized in another Christian denomination and have never been confirmed. Along with these changes, the 1979 Book of Common Prayer states that "Holy Baptism is appropriately administered within the Eucharist as the chief service on a Sunday or other feast."[22] Prior to this prayer book, in the Episcopal Church the regular practice was "private baptism" with only the parents and godparents or sponsors present.

The focus on the baptismal ministry of the laity, that baptism admits one fully into the life, worship, and ministry of the church, is the undergirding theology of the 1979 Book of Common Prayer.

---

21. Hatchett, *American Prayer Book*, 268.
22. *Book of Common Prayer*, 298.

As the baptismal rite says, through holy baptism by water and the Holy Spirit, the baptized share in the royal priesthood of Christ and, thus, participate in the life of God. The participation of all the baptized in the life, worship, and governance of the church, in the priesthood of Christ, makes them the fundamental ministers of the church. This was a new, perhaps even radical, sacramental practice for the Episcopal Church, and more broadly within the realm of Anglican practice of the time.

It is noteworthy that commentators have made this argument from various points of view, from those who supported the change in practice, and from those who did not. For example, Michael Ramsey, archbishop of Canterbury 1961–74, viewed the notion of holy baptism as full initiation as a new understanding within Anglicanism, which he says historically saw confirmation as completing the rite of initiation begun in baptism. In a lecture I heard in seminary, later edited into a book, Ramsey said,

> It does strain the unity of the Anglican Communion seriously when a particular Anglican Church veers off in some radical direction without the assurance of consensus, not caring or being cognizant always of the larger Anglican family. The two obvious issues are, of course, ordination and confirmation. It seems to me that a particular part of the Anglican Communion should not have made a total reevaluation of ordination and confirmation without a good deal of inter-Anglican consensus on the subjects. Please note what I am pleading for: not that the wisdom behind either is wrong, but that there should be more inter-Anglican consensus about those matters that are truly revolutionary in relation to Anglican union and witness in the world.[23]

Paul Avis, former general secretary of the Church of England's Council for Christian Unity, and theological consultant for the Anglican Communion, wrote,

> It is sometimes said that Baptism comprises the whole of sacramental initiation. This view, which I designate

---

23. Ramsey, *Anglican Spirit*, 114.

as "BACSI"—"Baptism as Complete Sacramental Initiation"—seems to have achieved the status of unquestioned orthodoxy in some circles. I am interested in the question of where it has come from, because it does not have support in the Eastern or Western traditions or in the Book of Common Prayer, 1662, and is in fact a late twentieth-century innovation.[24]

Avis goes on to say,

> In contrast to the American prayer book, I see Christian initiation as a process or journey—we could say an event that is extended over time for pastoral reasons—one that involves several sacramental milestones, including, crucially and fundamentally, Baptism. . . . But all that is contained in Baptism is received over time and Baptism does not stand alone as a means of inducting us into the life of grace in the church.[25]

On the side of those favoring the notion of holy baptism as full initiation were Charles Price and Louis Weil. In their 1980 book, published *in lieu* of an official publication from the Standing Liturgical Commission of the Episcopal Church, they say,

> The Protestant Reformation of the sixteenth century made one major attempt to restore worship along New Testament lines. A second such effort is going on before our eyes. . . .
>
> There is also a new insistence in our worship on the active participation of as many people in the congregation as possible. Perhaps this development has come about because we are learning to think of the church, as in the New Testament times, not as a building, not as clergy, but as the entire people of God, all with significant parts to play both in worship and in the life of the church in the world. . . . Perhaps it is also because at this distance the spontaneity of liturgical practice in the earliest Christian community looks so very attractive.[26]

24. Avis, "Baptism," 51.
25. Avis, "Baptism," 52.
26. Price and Weil, *Liturgy for Living*, 6.

BAPTISM AND EUCHARIST

Specifically, regarding the 1979 rite of holy baptism, they say,

> The new rite of Holy Baptism attempts to take our entire history into account to recognize that Anglican teaching about the nature of baptism depends on the whole development of Christian initiation in the life of the church. This long-range perspective faces us with ambiguities. There is no single, golden norm on which to model a new rite of baptism today. Around the simple act of pouring water, the church has clustered a variety of actions with a diversity of meanings. The fundamental principle underlying the rite of baptism in the current Prayer Book, however, is that "Holy Baptism is full initiation by water and the Holy Spirit into Christ's body, the Church." From New Testament times on, baptism has meant repentance, renunciation of an old way of life ("the world, the flesh, and the devil"), confession of faith in God, and a ritual participation in the death and resurrection of Christ. These meanings appear with greater or lesser clarity in every baptism liturgy. The current Book of Common Prayer makes these elements stand in particularly bold and clear relief for our time.[27]

Further, it appears that this sacramental practice will remain and perhaps be expanded upon in new rites that may be proposed for use in the Episcopal Church, as evidenced in guiding documents of the Task Force on Liturgical and Prayer Book Revision, established by the General Convention of the Episcopal Church.[28]

In a book written to inform church-wide study regarding new liturgical rites for the Episcopal Church, Jeffrey Lee has written,

> The Book of Common Prayer 1979 continues to shape the life of the Episcopal Church in profound ways that are ongoing. Chief among them are these: the insistence that Holy Baptism is the fundamental sacrament of ministry, that the celebration of the Holy Eucharist is the normative form of worship on the Lord's Day, that participation in the liturgy is the primary source of nourishment for Christian engagement with the world. These convictions

---

27. Price and Weil, *Liturgy for Living*, 76.
28. Task Force on Liturgical Prayer and Prayer Book Revision, "Principles."

endure even as new questions arise about prayer book revision for the twenty-first century and beyond. Indeed, the prayer book changes precisely in order to remain the same.[29]

It appears that within the official structures of the Episcopal Church, while there is work being done to revise worship, the notion of holy baptism by water and the Holy Spirit as full initiation into Christ's body the church will not only endure but continue to be foundational for future liturgies.

Some have described the changes in sacramental practice of the 1979 Book of Common Prayer as innovations in Anglicanism. Others maintain that a theology of the full participation of the baptized in the life of God and therefore the church have been present in Anglican theology all along, even if not fully reflected in official Anglican practice, such as requiring confirmation before being allowed to receive Holy Communion. I disagree with Ramsey, Avis, Price, and Weil that baptism as full initiation into the church is a new teaching. Following A. M. Allchin, I think a case can be made that the notion of the full participation of the baptized in the life of God and therefore in church has had a presence in Anglican theology since the English Reformation and, prior to 1979, was more of a forgotten theology than a new theology.[30]

While the 1979 Book of Common Prayer gives a renewed vision in Anglican life of the full participation of the baptized, it remains to be fulfilled in the life of the Episcopal Church. The full participation of the baptized in the life, worship, and governance of the church has yet to match the language of the Book of Common Prayer of 1979. Since 1979, studies show that attendance and membership in not only the Episcopal Church[31] but Christian denominations generally are declining numerically in the United States.[32]

---

29. Lee, *Spirit and Truth*, 26–27.
30. Allchin, *Participation in God*.
31. Episcopal Church, "Baptized Members."
32. Pew, "Religiously Unaffiliated."

On Sunday morning, congregations of many denominations and traditions continue a model of worship that does not allow for the full participation of the laity in the Lord's Supper as a meal. The consequence is that people do not fully experience participating in the worship of the church and, thus, do not experience participating in the wider life and mission of the church and, thus, do not experience more fully the life of the Triune God. To reduce the eucharistic meal to bread and wine alone is to minimize the experience of God as Creator of all food, to minimize the experience of God as sanctifier of all of creation and the produce of creation, and to minimize the experience of God as present in all food. When a person in holy orders is at a table with the only food being bread and wine, the priesthood of all the baptized is minimized and the abundance of God's loving providing of all food is reduced to something not seen as sacred. As Oliver points out, "From its origins, the eucharist was also a sign and evidence of a new world: the kingdom of God, already sprouting among us although its fullest consummation is still the come." Writing in the third century, Tertullian described that in a eucharistic meal "so much is eaten as satisfies hunger; as much drunk as is fitting for the pure. Appetite is satisfied to the extent appropriate for those who are mindful that they have to worship God even at night; they speak, as those who know the Master is listening."[33]

Reappropriating meals with the celebration of the Eucharist is a primary way of living into a participatory pattern of worship. Participatory worship with holy discourse and eucharistic meals encourages a reclaiming of vital and growing congregational life.

Meyers notes one place where worship with a meal occurs— Open Door in Atlanta. Open Door is a residential community in the Catholic Worker tradition where hospitality is offered to people on the street. They are offered "nourishment, place, safety, justice, friendship, and the knowledge of God's love and grace."[34] On Sunday afternoons the dining room is used for worship, which then flows into the evening meal. It is a model of Christian hospitality,

---

33. Oliver, "Banquet," 24.
34. Meyers, *Missional Worship*, 160.

Participation in God

yet it is based on a community intentionally set up to serve the poor. As wonderful as that ministry is, it has the practical effect still of making a separate room for the poor, not everyone sitting down as equals at the same table. Meyers, drawing on Craig Dykstra and Dorothy Bass, sees the eucharistic meal as multifaceted, holding together numerous biblical images of sacred meals. Dykstra and Bass underscore these connections: "We begin to understand that the family table, the table provided for the destitute, the table of holy communion, and the eschatological table where all people will feast in the fullness of God are not isolated from one another, but are part of a coherent whole constituted by the encompassing, unifying reality of God's active presence for the life of the world."[35]

To again return to the theme of the church as God's household, the eucharistic table is where all of the members of the household gather, side by side. The eucharistic meal table fulfills the vision of Isaiah,

> On this mountain the LORD of hosts will make for all peoples
>   a feast of rich food, a feast of well-aged wines,
>   of rich food filled with marrow, of well-aged wines strained clear.
> And he will destroy on this mountain
>   the shroud that is cast over all peoples,
>   the covering that is spread over all nations;
>   he will swallow up death forever.
> Then the Lord GOD will wipe away the tears from all faces,
>   and the disgrace of his people he will take away from all the earth,
>   for the LORD has spoken.
> It will be said on that day,
>   "See, this is our God; we have waited for him, so that he might save us.
>   This is the LORD for whom we have waited;
>   let us be glad and rejoice in his salvation."[36]

---

35. Dykstra and Bass, "Christian Practices," 29, quoted in Meyers, *Missional Worship*, 161.

36. Isa 25:6–9.

The table of the eucharistic meal is a continuation of the hospitality of Abraham and Sarah, serving all humanity, making all of us heirs of Abraham and Sarah as they fed wandering sojourners, heirs of Jesus Christ as he fed multitudes, and realizing the eschatological banquet on earth as it is in heaven.

"Nonreligious" organizations know that getting people to sit at a table together for a meal builds social capital, and smart organizations advocate for such practices more and more, such as is evident from this quote from the book *Never Eat Alone* by Keith Ferrazzi,

> Over the course of a few years, the retreats grew into a thriving event business called Summit Series, with both for-profit and nonprofit wings. Summit isn't just in the business of helping launch entrepreneurs. It's in the business of creating community, the most valuable form of social capital—the intimate, supportive relationships that spur collaboration while deeply satisfying our human need for connection, belonging, and meaning. Otherwise put, "a lifelong community of colleagues, contacts, friends, and mentors."[37]

The importance of social connections has been known in psychology for decades and is the focus of "intergroup contact theory."

> The basic premise of the contact hypothesis is that contact between individuals who belong to different groups can foster the development of more positive out-group attitudes. Why is the issue of intergroup contact so popular in social psychology research? A possible answer is that prejudice and conflict remain intractable characteristics of the societies in which we live, despite attempts of politicians and policymakers to successfully implement social change. As such, contact and its effectiveness at improving out-group attitudes has been an appealing and enduring research topic for social scientists.[38]

---

37. Ferrazzi, *Never Eat Alone*, loc. 86.
38. Vezzali and Stathi, *Contact Theory*, 1.

Participation in God

While I am not so naive as to think that church gatherings alone can solve the prejudice and conflicts in our country, as evidenced in Barbara F. Walters's book *How Civil Wars Start and How to Stop Them*, church gatherings around a eucharistic meal consisting of people from various walks of life—different political viewpoints, socioeconomic statuses, racial and ethnic backgrounds, sexual orientations, "all sorts and conditions of people"—could not only be a salve in our society but itself a very legitimate mission and ministry of the people of God.

Again, as the catechism in the 1979 Book of Common Prayer says, "The mission of the Church is to restore all people to unity with God and each other in Christ. . . . The ministry of lay persons is to represent Christ and his Church: to bear witness to him wherever they may be; and, according to the gifts given them, to carry on Christ's work of reconciliation in the world; and to take their place in the life, worship, and governance of the Church."[39]

This chapter began with looking at the church as God's household, and specifically looked at the roles of baptism and the Eucharist as the central ways God's household participates in God's life. I have attempted to make the case that a return to a full eucharistic meal is not only biblically and historically authentic but is also a worthy practice to restore as the church declines and as society fragments more and more.

Richard Hooker saw the Eucharist as nurturing us and bringing us closer to the life of God by degrees of glory, by lifelong transformation into the "full stature of Christ," as the baptismal liturgy says, quoting Eph 4:13. Growing from "one degree of glory to another" is a way of talking about changing to be more like God.

The phrase "transformed from one degree of glory to another" comes from 2 Cor 3:18. In this passage Paul is contrasting glory in Christianity and Judaism. The key difference between the two is Paul's interpretation of glory that is hidden and glory that is revealed to all. Moses' face is transformed by God's glory on Mt. Sinai, and God's glory is so bright that he has to cover his face. But as Jason Fout explains, there is a Jewish tradition that says over

---

39. *Book of Common Prayer*, 855.

time the glory faded from Moses' face, and he kept his face covered to hide the fading.

> In contrast, "all of us" see God's glory reflected in one another (v. 18a), an unfading glory which does not need hiding and which we do behold, unlike those who beheld the glory in Moses' face (v. 7), who were repelled by fear (Exod. 34.30). The "beholding" of the glory cannot be dispassionate, neutral, disengaged: the one who sees is transformed; the one who is transformed allows others to see (and be transformed). This transformation is "from glory to glory" (apó dóxhV eiV dóxan) or, "from one degree of glory to another" as the NRSV translates it, in a dynamic of ever-greater increase given by God.[40]

Fout points to Paul Ricoeur,

> In this way he forged the central metaphor of the Christian self as christomorphic, that is, the image of the image par excellence. A chain of glory, if we may put it this way—of descending glory, it must be added—is created in this way: God's glory, that of Christ, that of the Christian. At the far end of this chain, if the mediation goes back to the origin, the christomorphic self is both fully dependent and fully upstanding: an image "always more glorious," according to the apostle.[41]

This christomorphic life of continual transformation by one degree of glory to another is a central way of understanding the notion of growing into the full stature of Christ.

Richard Hooker connects baptism, Eucharist, and transformation with our participation in God. "The union or mutuall participation which is betweene Christ and the Church of Christ is in this present worlde," he says. In language that is rather graphic he defines participation as "that mutuall inward hold which Christ hath of us and wee of him, in such sorth that ech possesseth other by waie of special interest propertie and inherent copulation."[42]

---

40. Fout, *Fully Alive*, loc. 3897.
41. Fout, *Fully Alive*, loc. 3924.
42. Hooker, *Laws*, 234.

Chapter 57 of book V of Hooker's *Laws* is titled "The Necessitie of Sacraments unto the Participation of Christ." Hooker here sees that baptism and the Eucharist are participation in God and the means by which we are continually transformed, growing into the full stature of Christ.

> Wee receive Christ Jesus in baptisme once as the first beginner, in the Eucharist often as beinge by continewall degrees the finisher of our life. By baptism therefore wee receive Christ Jesus and from him that saving grace which is proper unto baptisme. By the other sacrament wee receive him also imparting therein him selfe and that grace which the Eucharist properlie bestoweth. So that ech sacrament having both that which is generall or common, and that also which is peculiar unto it selfe, wee maie herby gather that the participation of Christ which properlie belongeth to any one sacrament is not otherwise to be obtained by the sacrament whereunto it is proper.[43]

Hooker sees baptism as initiation, the beginning of a sacramental life, and he sees the Eucharist as a means of continual degrees of growth. Paul Dominiak explains,

> While baptism instrumentally imputes grace and begins sanctification, Hooker recognizes that the quotidian travails of sin mean that "wee are both subject to diminution and capable of augmentation in grace." The Eucharist helps believers grow by steps and degrees into grace and union with God: "such as will live the life of god must eate the fleshe and drinke the blood of the Sonne of Adam." Rather, for Hooker sanctification unfurls through time and materiality: Christ transforms the recipient of grace "by steppes and degrees" from sinfulness towards eschatological glory through the practices of the visible Church. Accordingly, sacramental participation forms the heart of the visible Church's activity. . . . Sanctification occurs (although is not guaranteed) through Eucharistic participation: the liturgical reception of Christ's

---

43. Hooker, *Laws*, 248.

body and blood is necessary for growth in grace, reconciling extrinsic justification with intrinsic sanctification as a prolepsis of eschatological glory. . . . Hooker's real concern in the Laws remains sanctification, the spiritual regeneration and growth of believers through the Holy Spirit in the visible Church. The goal of sanctification is participation in Christ.[44]

Still, even with God's grace, even with participating in God through our creaturehood, through partaking of God's creation, having our lives sustained, and the fullness of sacramental life and grace, adam the first and adam the second continue to live in us. While we put on the new Adam in baptism, it is also a daily task to reaffirm our baptismal promises, to grow into the full stature of Christ, to be transformed from one degree of glory to another. In short, it is hard to change.

There are any number of things most of us would like to change about the world and other people. But changing ourselves, especially to become more like Christ, and thus more us, as we were baptized to become, is another matter. For everyone in the church to change is perhaps more daunting, especially when one realizes no one can make anyone else change. To help, I will now turn to the subject of adaptive change.

---

44. Dominiak, *Richard Hooker*, 73, 160–62.

CHAPTER 5

Adaptive Change as Participation in God

IN THIS CHAPTER I will examine the place of adaptive change in the life of the church and how the work of adaptive change assists our transformation from one degree of glory to another, as we participate in God. I will raise again the notion of the two adams, particularly as they apply to the role of authority that can provide technical fixes and the role of leadership that deals with adaptive change. I will explain how change from one degree of glory to another informs and is informed by the work of adaptive change.

Ron Heifetz of the Kennedy School of Government at Harvard has written and taught extensively on the subject of adaptive leadership.[1] Heifetz makes a key distinction between authority and leadership. In every organization there are people who have authority. In the church this would include heads of denominations, judicatories and congregations, and clergy and laity with varying levels of authority. Authority is given to certain people based on training and qualification. Because authority is given, authority may also be removed. The purpose of authority in an organization is to provide direction, protection, and order.[2] People in authority solve problems by providing technical fixes. Technical fixes address problems for which there are established and recognizable solutions. In Soloveitchik's schema, adam the first is made to exercise authority, using magisterial power,rationality, and skill

---

1. Heifetz et al., *Adaptive Leadership*.
2. Heifetz et al., *Adaptive Leadership*, 28.

to efficiently provide the technical fixes of direction, protection, and order. Adam the first excels at rational problem solving and relishes using authority and power to solve them. Solving these problems is an essential part of the task of providing direction, protection, and order, and adam the first is the right person for the job. And it should be made clear, organizations need someone to work on solving technical problems. Adam the first authentically uses authority as a form of service to the community. While it the case that adam the second names the animals, this is a matter of relationship, both companionship and adam's dominion. This is still different than adam the first, whose orientation is less about relationship than providing authority—direction, protection, and order. Heifetz contrasts authority with leadership.

Unlike authority, leadership is not conferred, and may be exercised by anyone in an organization. On occasion problems present themselves in organizations that have no obvious answers, which cannot simply be solved by authority. These problems are called adaptive challenges. Often adaptive challenges are lying just beneath the surface of the life and culture of an organization. Privately, people may well know that there is a challenge in the community that is not easily solved and is beyond the ability of authority to provide a technical fix. When adaptive challenges do arise in the open conversation of a community, and the community is aware of these problems, it creates anxiety in the system. When anxiety occurs, people look to authority to relieve the anxiety as a way of providing direction, protection, and order. But providing ways of relieving the anxiety is not the same as solving the adaptive challenge. One of the mistakes people in authority often make is to try to sooth the anxiety with a technical fix rather than helping the system address the adaptive challenge. Or, if they know they cannot solve the adaptive challenge, sometimes people in authority simply do nothing because they think their only role, as a person in authority, is to solve problems.

By contrast, adaptive leadership is the practice of mobilizing people to tackle tough challenges and thrive.[3] Leadership is the

---

3. Heifetz et al., *Adaptive Leadership*, 14.

work of adam the second. Adam the second, largely because of the self-knowledge of his own fall and redemption, sees the adaptive challenges and knows that addressing those adaptive challenges will cause disruption, a sense of disequilibrium. Leadership is the ability to recognize and name the adaptive challenge, to gather the community together to address the challenge, and to listen and model the task of listening back to the community. The table below shows that problems do not always come in neat packages as either "technical" or "adaptive," and many problems are a mix of technical and adaptive challenges.

Figure 2: Distinguishing Technical Problems and Adaptive Challenges[4]

Kind of Challenge	Problem of Definition	Solution	Locus of Work
Technical	Clear	Clear	Authority
Technical and Adaptive	Clear	Requires Learning	Authority and Stakeholders
Adaptive	Requires Learning	Requires Learning	Stakeholders

According to Heifetz et al., adaptive challenges are hard for all communities because they involve an experience of loss, of brokenness. This does not mean that the community itself is a broken or dysfunctional community, in the sense that it needs to be repaired or cured. Rather, there is emotional brokenness when dealing with adaptive challenges. When people perceive that there is going to be a loss, they resist the change that will bring the loss. The loss occurs on several levels. First, there is a sense of loss and anxiety when there is a realization that the person in authority cannot solve all the problems. Second, there is loss when one realizes the work of adaptive change requires one's own energy and involvement. And the most challenging loss comes with the realization that not only do things have to change but one has to change oneself. When

---

4. Heifetz et al., *Adaptive Leadership*, 20.

the community becomes conscious that there are no easy answers there is a dawning sense of disequilibrium.

This is a daunting time for people in systems that rely heavily on authority because people look to authority to keep equilibrium, not to allow disequilibrium, and certainly not to encourage disequilibrium. It may seem at first that, in Heifetz's model, exercising authority and exercising adaptive leadership are almost opposite roles, with opposite expectations. But Heifetz does see ways that people in authority may exercise adaptive leadership. When people in authority exercise adaptive leadership he describes it as "dancing on the edge of authority."

FIGURE 3: LEADERSHIP FROM A
POSITION OF AUTHORITY[5]

Task	Technical	Adaptive
Direction	Provide problem definition and solution	Identify the adaptive challenge; frame key questions and issues
Protection	Protect from external threats	Disclose external threats
Order:		
Orientation	Orient people to current roles	Disorient current roles; resist orienting people to new roles too quickly
Conflict	Restore order	Expose conflict or let it emerge
Norms	Maintain norms	Challenge norms or let them be challenged

All of this requires that the people in authority enter messy disequilibrium with their community. "To practice adaptive leadership, you have to help people navigate through a period of disturbance as they sift through what is essential and what is expendable, and as they experiment with solutions to the adaptive challenges at hand."[6] The theological reference here is the incarnation. When

5. Heifetz et al., *Adaptive Leadership*, 28.
6. Heifetz et al., *Adaptive Leadership*, 28.

God entered human life God entered the messy disequilibrium and chaos of sinful humanity generally, and into the specific historical context of first-century, Roman-occupied Palestine.

As Jesus emptied himself, taking the form of a servant, for someone in authority to exercise adaptive leadership means that the person in authority is willing to let go some of the usual decision-making roles. Depending on the tradition, there are times when clergy particularly feel that this is almost a violation of their rights and/or responsibilities. In situations where authority has clear answers to defining and solving a problem, this is true. But when there is the presence of an adaptive challenge it becomes necessary to share the authority so that leadership may happen. The person in authority will still be exercising authority when that person oversees the process of addressing and solving an adaptive challenge. It should be seen as a role of presiding over the process, not of deciding alone how to solve the adaptive challenge but creating a space where the process may unfold. Heifetz calls this the "productive zone of disequilibrium."[7]

FIGURE 4: PRODUCTIVE ZONE OF DISEQUILIBRIUM[8]

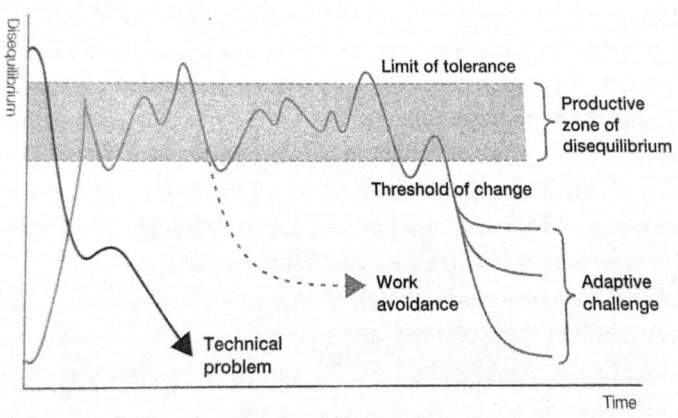

7. Heifetz et al., *Adaptive Leadership*, 30.

8. This graph is taken from *Adaptive Leadership*. Heifetz et al., *Adaptive Leadership*, 50.

Adaptive Change as Participation in God

The art of adaptive leadership is "keeping a hand on the thermostat," according to Heifetz.[9] First, there is no blaming of people for the anxiety they are feeling; anxiety about fear of losing something important is real and even appropriate. Here, the people with authority must engage their compassionate sensibilities and practices, even as they let go of the formal organizational authority. There must be an acknowledgment that there is pain in change, and those in authority who want to lead adaptive change must have compassion for those who are experiencing it. The purpose of addressing adaptive change is not explicitly to make people anxious or to blame them for their anxiety. That there are people feeling anxiety may be a consequence of adaptive change, but it is not the purpose. One of the things that people may find most disturbing is that they are bearing some responsibility for solving a problem that has no obvious answers in a community they care about.

It is very likely the case that there have been long simmering issues in the life of the community, and these may be on the verge of being exposed publicly. All of this produces a certain amount of heat. The productive zone of disequilibrium is similar to a cooking pot. In order to get the right solution, in order for the adaptive work to happen, there has to be willingness to live with some heat. If the temperature gets too high it will not only damage or possibly destroy the process, but it may also damage or destroy the community and the person in authority with it.

Once adaptive work begins there are no clear, straight paths to follow. Adaptive change comes in fits and starts, going forward and backwards, trying out various things and taking them on, unclear whether a particular solution has been found until it has been tried. Because adaptive work is so trying and because it means loss for the community, there will inevitably be various means employed to avoid the work.

The most classic and dangerous is to blame the authority—the clergy and/or lay leaders in the case of the church—for the

---

9. Heifetz et al., *Adaptive Leadership*, 49.

fact that there is an adaptive challenge at all. "A good leader would know how to lead us out of this and would know how to provide the answers," people might say. There may indeed be a movement to remove the person in authority, which is an excellent way to avoid the work of adaptive change and puts all of the focus on getting a new person in authority who people believe can solve the community's problems. Other ways of avoiding the work are playing around with structures, physical and human, in the belief that this will solve, or at least distract attention from, the adaptive challenge. All too often, committees end up being charged to solve an adaptive challenge with technical fixes. Frequently, after much study, recommendations are made, some policies or practices are put in place, but the adaptive challenge remains because the community as a whole has not done adaptive work. Adaptive work is messy work.

The person or people leading adaptive change need to attend to people's hearts, but they also need to be self-differentiated enough that they have will and stamina to stay with the process. In particular, Heifetz says that adaptive leadership requires three key activities: "(1) observing events and patterns around you; (2) interpreting what you are observing (developing multiple hypotheses about what is really going on); and (3) designing interventions based on the observations and interpretations to address the adaptive challenge you have identified."[10]

Observation means getting off of the "dance floor and getting on the balcony" to see the whole and serve the whole, to watch oneself as well as others while one is in the action, and to see patterns of what is happening that are hard to see at ground level.[11] From a Christian perspective it is about imagining the view of God from the perch of heaven. How does what we are doing, including what I am doing, look to God? It is about making things on earth as they are in heaven. It means being "wise as a serpent and innocent as a dove." An acute observer will ask, "Who is talking with

10. Heifetz, et al., *Adaptive Leadership*, 32.
11. Heifetz, et al., *Adaptive Leadership*, 32.

Adaptive Change as Participation in God

whom? Who is responding to whom? What groups and alliances are being formed? What is the history of this adaptive challenge? What are the patterns of behavior relevant to the problem that are not visible unless you're looking for them? How are the community's culture and structures affecting people's behavior?"[12]

Interpretation is even more difficult than observation. When a person leading an adaptive challenge offers an interpretation there is a risk that others will have another interpretation, and they will resent the person leading. The truth is people are hard wired to make interpretations, and most interpretations are made unconsciously at great speed. The natural impulse is to act on our interpretations. It is better to sit for a while with one's interpretation before acting. It is quite appropriate to question one's own interpretation and to ask if there are other hypotheses. Still, even the most considered interpretations will be good guesses unless one has all the data, and no one person is capable of knowing and evaluating all of the possible interpretations. It is even wise to hold one or more interpretations in one's head at once even if they are contradictory. When the leader of adaptive change is ready to intervene, it is time to share one's interpretation, and it will be provocative. "Making it tentatively, experimentally, and then watching (and then interpreting) the reaction can help you gauge how close to the mark you came."[13]

The intervention itself should be seen as an experiment by the leader and all the stakeholders and should be in the service of a shared purpose. If the community cannot see the relevance, there is a risk that the intervention will be dismissed as the leader's own issue or cause rather than something that pertains to the whole community. The intervention should also be based on the resources of the community. It is appropriate and even necessary when people in authority are considering an intervention in an adaptive challenge to be mindful of their own skills and personal

---

12. Heifetz, et al., *Adaptive Leadership*, 33.
13. Heifetz, et al., *Adaptive Leadership*, 35.

Participation in God

resources. It is entirely appropriate to ask, What am I good at? Am I the right person to lead this kind of intervention?

Continuing to find solutions to adaptive challenges requires experimentation and risk. Even defining the adaptive challenge may be risky. It means trying interventions and being willing to accept their failure and then trying again, without being defensive about the failure. "In the realm of adaptive leadership, you have to believe that your intervention is absolutely the right thing to do at the moment you commit to it. But at the same time, you need to remain open to the possibility that you are dead wrong."[14]

Leading adaptive change requires compassion for those in the community, courage of heart, and skill in learning new competencies. The person leading adaptive change must connect with the values, beliefs, and anxieties of the people in the community, being present with one's heart laid open to the people. Adaptive change is not about persuading people logically or through arguments about facts. It is not adam the first's work. People cannot be argued rationally into adaptive change. "They are stuck in their hearts and stomachs, not in their heads. To move them, you need to reach them there. If you are not engaged with your own heart, you will find it virtually impossible to connect with their hearts."[15] Leading adaptive change means being fully aware of one's own adam the first and adam the second tendencies. It means knowing how and when to be an adam the first rationalist, and how and when to be an adam the second compassionate. It requires suppleness with one's own self-image, and suppleness in how and what to communicate and how and what to ask.

Further, in the church we have a resource not always acknowledged in other communities. That is the belief and conviction that God is with us. Church authorities can help the congregation remember how it began, and that God has been with that community from the beginning in various iterations. They can remind the community of Jesus' own willingness to suffer and die before

---

14. Heifetz, et al., *Adaptive Leadership*, 37.
15. Heifetz, et al., *Adaptive Leadership*, 39.

Adaptive Change as Participation in God

having resurrected life and that Jesus will be with the community as it dies and rises again. The community can remember that while this is a time for breaking, it is also a time to consider what part of the original DNA is worth taking into the future. Authorities exercising leadership can remind the community that while Jesus was crucified, it was the same Jesus who was resurrected, with the same body, wounds and all. And they can assure the community that even with radical change and loss, it will be recognizable and will still be itself, although in a new life.

Still, even if a community really gets to the point of wanting to make an adaptive change, it may fail to do so, no matter how much it wants it. Robert Kegan and Lisa Laskow Lahey believe that they have discovered that people have an "immunity to change."[16] Their research shows that change is not simply a matter of changing behaviors. Their point is that all of us have an emotional immune system to keep us safe and alive. Immune systems are generally good things. But sometimes immune systems cause problems, such as rejecting new material, internal or external to the body; the immune system can put us in danger. The immune system is not intending danger; it is simply making a mistake. It must alter its code.[17] And when it comes to emotions, our immune system's primary job is to manage anxiety, which Kegan and Lahey believe is the "most important and least understood—private emotion in public life."[18] While our emotional immune systems work at lowering our anxiety, unconsciously to us, they can also create blind spots, preventing new learning and constantly constraining action in some aspects of our living.

> It is change that leaves us feeling defenseless before the dangers we "know" to be present that causes anxiety. Overturning an immunity to change always raises the specter of leaving us exposed to such dangers. We build

---

16. Kegan and Lahey, *Immunity*, 10.
17. Kegan and Lahey, *Immunity*, 64.
18. Kegan and Lahey, *Immunity*, 78.

an immune system to save our lives. We are not easily going to surrender such a critical protection.[19]

In their work Kegan and Lahey create a simple way of understanding our immunity to change, what they call an X-ray of one's immunity to change. Individually and communally we may have (1) visible commitments, such as losing weight; (2) things that we are doing or not doing instead, such as eating too much, eating when not hungry, eating the wrong kinds of food; and (3) hidden competing commitments, such as not being bored (given food is one of the pleasures of life), not feeling empty, eating socially to connect with people, etc. Finally, these commitments are (4) based on big assumptions, such as I need food to keep from being bored, I have no other pleasures in life, or I cannot socialize without sharing food. It is these hidden competing commitments that keep us from changing, and they are so strong that we have anxiety that they may be threatened. Consequently, our emotional immune systems protect us and keep us from changing. Our hidden competing commitments are just that; they are hidden and unconscious.[20]

Kegan offers a way of addressing this that is consistent with his decades-long commitment to human developmental theory and that is consistent with the general case I am making in this book: participation in life with God involves being transformed from one degree of glory to another. Kegan's model for overcoming immunity to change is shown below.[21]

---

19. Kegan and Lahey, *Immunity*, 80.
20. Kegan and Lahey, *Immunity*, 125–67.
21. Kegan and Lahey, *Immunity*, 84.

Adaptive Change as Participation in God

Figure 5: Self-Transforming Mind[22]

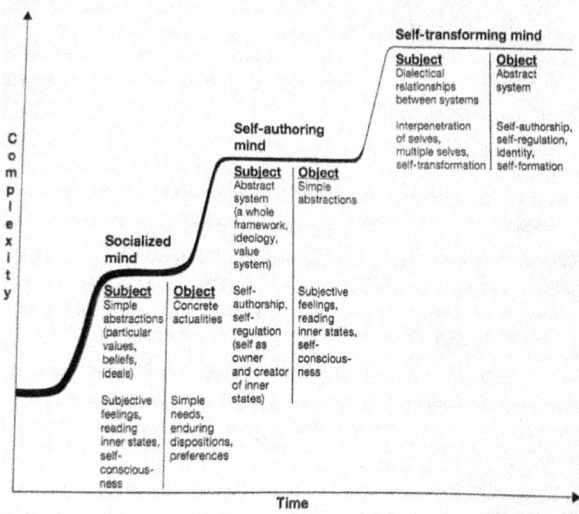

In this model, a person who perceives the world through a socialized mind is limited by the values and expectations of that person's nearest community, whether it is family, religious group, political affiliation, etc. At this level people may be assigned or encouraged to fulfill certain roles based on gender, race, or sexual orientation. Every culture has its own nuances and values about things as diverse as smiling or not smiling, shaking hands or not shaking hands, when and how to eat. To engage in adaptive change across cultures requires openness and learning across those cultures in a mutually open way. One current global adaptive challenge, climate change and how to address it, is perhaps the most vexing for these very reasons. It is much easier to think that some entities need to provide technical fixes than that everyone on earth needs to change, yet not all change in the same ways.

The perceived risks and dangers here are the possibility of being excluded from that community or being evaluated poorly

---

22. This graph of the self-transforming mind is taken from *Immunity to Change*. Kegan and Lahey, *Immunity*, 84.

by those whose opinion directly applies to one's opinion of oneself. At the level of the self-authoring mind, one can distinguish the views of others from one's self-opinion. Someone at this level will consider others' views but choose how much and in what way one will be influenced. Here, risk and anxiety are no longer about being excluded from one's community, but about falling short of one's own standards, being unable to realize one's agenda, losing control of one's life.

In the self-transforming mind, one moves beyond one's own "theory, system, script, framework, or ideology, one needs to develop an even more complex way of knowing that permits one to look *at*, rather than choicelessly *through* one's own framework."[23] This is that stage of liberation, where one is able to begin to see themselves as God's beloved child, first and foremost, and all other assigned roles lose their grip—whether from family, tribe, race, gender, or sexual orientation. When this happens, the framework becomes more an in-process way of looking rather than an ultimate reality. "This breaks through to a bigger emotional and mental space that can seek out the framework's current limitations rather than merely defend the current draft as a finished product and regard all suggestions to the contrary as a blow to the self."[24] In other words, this way of knowing lowers the threshold of anxiety; it reduces fear. Or, better put, it allows one to consider new life fearlessly.

Kegan and Lahey call this process "increasing mental complexity." They acknowledge the messiness of this process and that it involves the head and the heart, thinking and feeling. What increases mental complexity?

> If we were to summarize the answer that arises from seventy-five years of research on the question—begun long before our time in the laboratories of developmental psychologists like Jean Piaget and Barbel Inhelder in Switzerland or James Mark Baldwin, Heinz Werner, and

---

23. Kegan and Lahey, *Immunity*, 84.
24. Kegan and Lahey, *Immunity*, 84–85.

Adaptive Change as Participation in God

Lawrence Kohlberg in the United States—it would be *optimal conflict*.[25]

"Optimal conflict" consists of the (1) persistent experience of a frustration, dilemma, or personal problem, (2) perfectly designed to cause one to feel the limits of current ways of knowing, (3) in a part of life that one cares about, with (4) sufficient support so that one is neither overwhelmed by the conflict, nor able to escape or diffuse it.[26] When an individual or community does a full X-ray of one's immunity to change, it produces an optimal conflict. This takes the notion that a contradiction within a person or a community is what the community *is*, which is why the goal to change cannot be achieved, and converts it into a contradiction that a person or a community *has*, which can now be worked on. The contradiction that keeps change from happening goes from being seen as an essential and necessary part of identity, to being something the identity can stand apart from and change.

To connect Heifetz et al. with Kegan and Lahey, when a person in authority wants to engage in an intervention, Kegan and Lahey's X-ray of immunity to change is an excellent tool. The person who intends to lead adaptive change should do the exercise first, to test their own willingness and their own assumptions about who they are. If this person is the one with the most authority, then it would be good to do it next with a board or others who also exercise authority. Then, and this is risky but necessary, invite the whole community to the same process. Begin with getting people to answer the question, What is our goal? Just coming up with a consensus to that question may take some time, and it will help clarify what the adaptive challenge is. Then ask, What are we doing or not doing that keeps us from achieving our goal? Again, be prepared for some disagreement and perhaps some finger pointing. But don't let the group scapegoat onto anyone. Third, ask, What hidden commitments do we have that keep us doing or not doing

---

25. Kegan and Lahey, *Immunity*, 86 (italics original).
26. Kegan and Lahey, *Immunity*, 86.

what we need to do to achieve our goal? Finally ask, What are the big assumptions behind our competing commitments?

In the exercise of increasing mental complexity, one goes from looking at oneself as understood by a particular group or community to looking at oneself based on how one relates to a particular group or community to finally looking at oneself as one actually is and is therefore able to let go of the things that keep one from being who one truly is.

Kegan and Lahey's process of "embracing mental complexity" through optimal conflict is embedded in the Book of Common Prayer, in the baptismal liturgy and in the Eucharist. When we are baptized, and then when we renew our baptismal vows, we are reminded of what is primary about who we are. We promise once again to do things we have failed to do. In the confession and absolution of the Eucharist we acknowledge both the things we have done against God "in thought, word, and deed, and . . . what we have left undone."[27] Yet the act of confession also requires a "self-transforming mind," seeing that while we do sin, we are not our sins. We remain baptized members of the household of God and looking at ourselves in new ways helps us become ourselves in new ways. What both adam the first and adam the second have in common is agency. The most powerful way to use the agency given to us by God is to willfully change by continually offering ourselves to be transformed through the power of the Holy Spirit. It is to be like Jesus in willfully offering ourselves to God over and over again—not the image of ourselves given to us by any other group or social unit, not the image we have crafted in our own limited perspective, but the image of ourselves as we are made in God's image and baptized into his body.

This is another way of describing the process of growing from one degree of glory to another. One's view of oneself is no longer defined by others or by how we see ourselves based on our relationships with others. Rather, one sees oneself in the complex ways that God sees us, beloved and purposeful yet flawed and fumbling children of God—capable of being perfect, not in the ways that

---

27. *Book of Common Prayer*, 60.

the world or others would want us to be perfect but perfect in the ways that God wants us to be perfect, merely perfectly ourselves. Hooker has his own way of describing this process, which is quite helpful. Dominiak describes it this way,

> Faith is also an infused "intellectual habit of the mind" with her "seate in the understandinge" gifted at baptism and which intrinsically transforms the cognitive capacity of believers through sanctifying grace to participate supernaturally in God and enjoy salvific (re)union. Hooker obviates hyper-rationalism and clearly accounts for how sanctifying grace transforms cognitive capacities without recourse to an intractable form of irrationalism.[28]

In this process one escapes from the hyper-rationalism and technical problem solving of Adam the first and allows for sanctifying grace, and yet neither does one embrace irrationality. By increasing mental complexity, we embrace our own internal "optimal conflicts," and as communities we move in messy and uncertain ways into higher levels of being the authentic household God calls us to be, all empowered by the Holy Spirit.

Family systems theory shows us that households are rarely neat and tidy, that optimal conflict and things running beneath the surface are more usual than not in households. And yet family households are able to address adaptive challenges, and the first breakthrough moment is often when people begin to use "I statements" when discussing change and how one could change, rather than the fruitless practice of telling others how they need to change. This is consistent with the theory presented here by Kegan and Lahey. The very practice of using "I statements" opens up the notion that "I" need to change.

Dan Hardy describes this process through what he calls "temporal abduction,"

> which means allowing our imaginations to be drawn forward by divine attraction: an ongoing process of envisioning and re-envisioning, so that we are stretched forward by the divine purposes. This openness has its

28. Dominiak, *Richard Hooker*, 110.

source in something very deep within Anglicanism. In Richard Hooker's terms, it is to emphasize the fullness of God within the divine purposes, which is to allow oneself to be moved forward by God: moved forward in imagination, in mode of behaviour, in one's mode of reasoning and in one's sociality. Temporal abduction is a temporal movement of the Spirit: an abduction that grabs you into the spirit's wind and pulls you along in the direction of the divine movement: "The spirit blows where it chooses; you hear the sound of it, but you don't know where it comes from or where it is going" (John 3.8).[29]

For individuals and communities this can be liberating. How many things do communities think they ought to do as part of their lives, usually based on how things were done decades ago? How many communities decide they are successful or not based on how they compare to other communities? Instead, the questions should be, Who is this community really? What are this community's real gifts and strengths? What parts of this communal DNA are of God and worthy of carrying into the future without apology? When communities can let go of impossible, unreal, and burdensome expectations, then they are liberated to move into a new life. Individuals and communities can look at their past, give thanks for the ways in which they have been taken and blessed in countless ways over the years, acknowledge the current brokenness and the need for brokenness yet to come, and yet still anticipate resurrection, new life in this world, with the same flesh and the same bones, but new life, nonetheless.

All of this process is more easily attained when the community has developed habits of honest and open conversation before the work of adaptive challenges are presented. When God's household has the habit of gathering at table, sharing the body and blood of Christ, sharing food and wine from the earth, sharing berakah, then the church has a reservoir of social capital that gives it more power to do the work of adaptive change. If it has done the work of knowing each other, knowing their adam the first gifts of

---

29. Hardy et al., *Wording a Radiance*, loc. 1653.

intelligence, rationality, and power and knowing their adam the second gifts of redemption, compassion, and love, they will experience more willingness to be the sacrificial body of Christ on earth now.

Then the church will be heirs of the faith of Abraham and Sarah, offering hospitality to strangers, drawing the multitudes to the font and the table, and realizing the eschatological banquet on earth as it is in heaven. And as with Abraham and Sarah, all the Adam the first longings of having descendants as numerous as the stars and a place to abide on earth will be fulfilled as well. Then their individual and communal loneliness will be relieved, because old adam had died and new Adam is incarnate in his household, the church. Then the church glorifies God, and God is glorified in us. As Michael Ramsey wrote,

> [Adam] is transformed into the image of Christ, so as to become like unto Christ's perfect humanity, 1 Cor 15:49, 2 Cor 3:18, Rom 8:28, Col 3:9–10. In Christ [adam] is allowed to see not only the radiance of God's glory but also the true image of [adam]. Into that image Christ's people are now being transformed, and in virtue of this transformation into the new [Adam] they are realizing the meaning of their original status as creatures in God's image.
>
> Thus redemption is wrought not *in vacuo* but on the groundwork of creation. Through the work of Christ [adam] becomes what [adam] essentially is.... In Christ there is our human nature fulfilling both its true affinity to the creator and its true dependence upon Him in adoration; and the more we are brought to share in Christ's glory the more shall we share in that giving glory to the Father which was His mission and is our calling.[30]

---

30. Ramsey, *Glory and Transfiguration*, 151.

Postscript

Taste and See That the Lord Is Good

IN THESE PAGES I have advocated for seeing that all food is a sign of God's love in creation, and that the Eucharist should return to its origins as a full meal. In this postscript I would like to write about how all of us may enhance our experience of enjoying the fruits of God's creation and our labor when we partake of food and beverage, thus literally experiencing God's love in every bite and sip. While there may be some concern about gluttony and drunkenness, the truth is most people eat and drink more slowly and consume less when they slow down enough to taste and see.

What follows is based on talks that I give multiple times every week in my role as a wine advisor when I lead food and wine paired tastings. While some may interpret this as something that one would only apply in eating gourmet food and fine wine, my personal experience is that these practices work with all food and all beverages. I use these practices with everything from fine dining to granola bars and coffee. I do all of this briefly at the altar every time I preside at the Eucharist with the delicious bread and great wine at the church I serve, and I suggest that all who receive Holy Communion do the same. All of what follows is meant to encourage the practice of savoring food and beverage with everything we eat and drink. Savoring food and beverage requires slowing down and practicing mindfulness.

When one gets a beverage, take a minute or two to just look at it. Pick up the container and let light play with the beverage

Postscript

inside. Next, bring the drink to your nose and smell the beverage slowly through the nose. Next, if you have room in your beverage container, swirl the beverage vigorously. Swirling a beverage introduces oxygen into the beverage and helps it open up so that one can smell more. The safest way is to keep the container flat on a surface and swirl it. After swirling bring the drink to the nose again and breath in slowly. Some beverages are also enhanced by breathing in through the mouth. Next take a sip of the beverage but don't swallow it immediately. Swish the beverage around in the mouth enough so that it covers all of the taste buds. Only then, swallow the beverage and then again breathe in slowly through the mouth. Our tongues smell and taste, and this allows one to taste and smell simultaneously.

Now to the food: similar to a beverage, when first getting food, take a few moments to just look at it. I am somewhat notorious for getting my food at eye level, either by picking it up, or more often by getting my face on the same level as the food on the table. Feel free to rotate a plate or bowl so that the light may show different textures and shades of the food. Next, and this is very important, smell the food. That's right—smell the food. Depending on the food I will either put some food on a fork or spoon and bring it to my nose, or I may again either lift the whole plate or bowl to my nose, or I may do a face plant and lower my nose down to the food to smell it. Then take a bite but do not swallow it immediately. Chew it up thoroughly. Then after chewing the food thoroughly, squish it around in your mouth. Make sure all of the food has covered every part of the inside of your mouth. Then swallow, and as with the beverage, breathe in slowly through the mouth.

Now comes the most important part: the absolute best place to pair food and beverage is simultaneously in the mouth. First, follow the process above for a beverage. Then follow the process above for food, except, after thoroughly chewing the food take a sip of the beverage and let it stew with the food while all of it is in the mouth. Squish it around all over the mouth. Then swallow and breathe in slowly through the mouth. When food and beverage are paired simultaneously one is not merely combining flavors, but creating whole new flavors that only happen with that particular food and beverage. It is miraculous! It is a fulfillment of the prayer after a baptism, that the newly baptized know "the gift of joy and wonder in all your works," particularly God's most basic gifts of food and beverage.[1] The Book of Common Prayer wonderfully combines the notion of berakah and enjoyment of food and beverage in this prayer for blessing of a meal, "Blessed are you, O Lord God, King of the Universe, for you give us food to sustain our lives and make our hearts glad; through Jesus Christ our Lord. Amen."[2]

FIGURE 6

Maundy Thursday Liturgy, St. Paul's Church, Syracuse, New York, 2015

1. *Book of Common Prayer*, 308.
2. *Book of Common Prayer*, 835.

Bibliography

Allchin, A. M. *Participation in God: A Forgotten Strand in Anglican Tradition.* Wilton, CT: Morehouse-Barlow, 1988.
The American Heritage Dictionary. 5th ed. Boston: Houghton Mifflin Harcourt, 2015.
Arthur, Kate. "Adam McKay on the Ending(s) of 'Don't Look Up': DiCaprio's Last-Minute Line, Streep's Improv and Brontarocs." *Variety*, Dec. 27, 2021. https://variety.com/2021/film/news/adam-mckay-dont-look-up-ending-spoilers-1235142363/.
Attridge, Harold W., and Wayne A. Meeks, eds. *HarperCollins Study Bible.* New York: Harper Collins, 1993.
Avis, Paul. "Baptism and the Journey of Christian Initiation." In *Drenched in Grace: Essays in Baptismal Ecclesiology Inspired By the Work and Ministry of Louis Weil,* edited by Lizette Larson-Miller and Walter Knowles, 50–60. Eugene, OR: Pickwick, 2013.
Baker, Anthony D. *Diagonal Advance: Perfection in Christian Theology.* Eugene, OR: Cascade, 2011.
Bass, Diana Butler. *Christianity After Religion: The End of Church and the Birth of a New Spiritual Awakening.* New York: HarperCollins, 2012.
Bass, Dorothy C., ed. *Practicing Our Faith: A Way of Life for a Searching People.* San Francisco: Jossey-Bass, 1997.
The Book of Common Prayer. "Of the Administracion of Publyke Baptisme to Be Used in the Churche." The Book of Common Prayer, 1549. http://justus.anglican.org/resources/bcp/1549/Baptism_1549.htm.
Bradshaw, Paul F. *Early Christian Worship: A Basic Introduction to Ideas and Practice.* Collegeville, MN: Liturgical Press, 2010.
———. *Eucharistic Origins.* New York: Oxford University Press, 2004.
Bradshaw, Paul F., and Lawrence A. Hoffman, eds. *Life Cycles in Jewish and Christian Worship.* Notre Dame: University of Notre Dame Press, 1996.
Bradshaw, Paul F., and Maxwell E. Johnson. *The Eucharistic Liturgies.* Collegeville, MN: Liturgical Press, 2012.
Breyfogle, Todd. "Time and Transformation: A Conversation with Rowan Williams." *CrossCurrents* 45 (Fall 1995) 293–311.

Bibliography

Brown, David. *Divine Humanity: Kenosis and the Construction of a Christian Theology*. Waco, TX: Baylor University Press, 2011.

Brueggemann, Walter. *Genesis*. Interpretation. Louisville: Westminster John Knox, 1982. Kindle.

Burns, Stephen, ed. *Liturgical Spirituality: Anglican Reflections on the Church's Prayer*. New York: Seabury, 2013.

Christensen, Michael J., and Jeffrey A. Wittung. *Partakers of the Divine Nature: The History and Development of Deification in the Christian Traditions*. Grand Rapids: Baker Academic, 2008.

Coakley, Sarah. *The New Asceticism: Sexuality, Gender and the Quest for God*. London: Bloomsbury, 2015. Kindle.

Cohen, Shaye J. D. Galatians. In *The Jewish Annotated New Testament: Revised Standard Version*, edited by Amy Jill-Levine and Marc Zvi Brettler. New York: Oxford University Press, 2011.

Cook, Michael. Philippians. In *The Jewish Annotated New Testament: Revised Standard Version*, edited by Amy Jill-Levine and Marc Zvi Brettler. New York: Oxford University Press, 2011.

Curry, Michael B. *Crazy Christians: A Call to Follow Jesus*. New York: Morehouse, 2013.

Davison, Andrew. *Blessing*. Faith Going Deeper. Norwich: Canterbury Press, 2014. Kindle.

Dickinson, Colby. *Theology as Autobiography: The Centrality of Confession, Relationship, and Prayer to the Life of Faith*. Eugene, OR: Cascade, 2020.

Dominiak, Paul Anthony. *Richard Hooker: The Architecture of Participation*. London: T&T Clark Bloomsbury, 2020.

Drew, Mark. Introduction to *Consecrations, Blessings and Prayers: A Pastoral Companion to the Ritual and to the Book of Blessings*, by Sean Finnegan, 1–21. Rev. ed. Norwich: Canterbury Press, 2018.

Dudley, Carl S., and Nancy T. Ammerman. *Congregations in Transition: A Guide for Analyzing, Assessing, and Adapting in Changing Communities*. San Francisco: Jossey-Bass, 2002.

Dykstra, Craig, and Dorothy C. Bass. "A Theological Understanding of Christian Practices." In *Practicing Theology: Beliefs and Practices in Christian Life*, edited by Miroslav Volf and Dorothy C. Bass, 13–32. Grand Rapids: Eerdmans, 2001.

Episcopal Church. "The Episcopal Church: Baptized Members by Province and Diocese 2011–2020." https://extranet.generalconvention.org/staff/files/download/30689.

Ferrazzi, Keith. *Never Eat Alone*. New York: Currency, 2014. Kindle.

Fout, Jason A. *Fully Alive: The Glory of God and the Human Creature in Karl Barth, Hans Urs von Balthasar and Theological Exegesis of Scripture*. London: Bloomsbury T&T Clark, 2015. Kindle.

———. *Learning from London: Church Growth in Unlikely Places*. Cincinnati: Forward Movement, 2018.

BIBLIOGRAPHY

Fowler, James. *Stages of Faith: The Psychology of Human Development and the Quest for Meaning*. New York: HarperOne, 1995.

Fowler, James, and Sam Keen. *Life Maps: Conversations on the Journey of Faith*. Waco: Word, 1978.

Gorman, Michael J. *Inhabiting the Cruciform God: Kenosis, Justification, and Theosis in Paul's Narrative Soteriology*. Grand Rapids: Eerdmans, 2009.

Guilbert, Charles Mortimer, custodian. *The Book of Common Prayer and Administration of the Sacraments and Other Rites and Ceremonies of the Church*. New York: Church Publishing, 1979.

Hardy, Daniel W., and David F. Ford. *Jubilate: Theology in Praise*. London: Darton, Longman & Todd, 1984.

Hardy, Daniel W., et al. *Wording a Radiance: Parting Conversations on God and the Church*. London: SCM, 2010. Kindle.

Hatchett, Marion J. *Commentary on the American Prayer Book*. New York: Seabury, 1980.

Heifetz, Ronald, et al. *The Practice of Adaptive Leadership: Tools and Tactics for Changing Your Organization and the World*. Boston: Harvard Business, 2009.

Hooker, Richard. *The Works of Richard Hooker: Of the Laws of Ecclesiastical Polity*. Vol. 2. Folger Library Edition. Cambridge: Harvard University Press, 1977.

Hudock, Barry. *The Eucharistic Prayer: A User's Guide*. Collegeville, MN: Liturgical, 2010.

Kegan, Robert. *The Evolving Self*. Cambridge: Harvard University Press, 1982.

Kegan, Robert, and Lisa Laskow Lahey. *Immunity to Change: How to Overcome and Unlock the Potential in Yourself and Your Organization*. Boston: Harvard Business, 2009.

Kreglinger, Gisela H. *The Spirituality of Wine*. Grand Rapids: Eerdmans, 2016.

LaVerdiere, Eugene. *The Breaking of the Bread*. Chicago: Liturgy Training, 1998.

———. *Dining in the Kingdom of God*. Chicago: Liturgy Training, 1994.

Lee, Jeffrey. "Changing to Remain the Same." In *Spirit and Truth: A Vision of Episcopal Worship*, edited by Stephanie A. Budwey et al., 15–26. New York: Church Publishing, 2020. Kindle.

Macquarrie, John. *In Search of Humanity*. London: SCM Press, 1982.

———. *Principles of Christian Theology*. 2nd ed. New York: Scribner's Sons, 1977.

Mann, Alice. *The In-Between Church: Navigating Size Transitions in Congregations*. Washington, DC: Alban, 1998.

Marshall, Michael, and Edna Mary. *A Pattern of Faith*. London: Hodder & Stoughton, 1966.

McGowan, Andrew B. *Ancient Christian Worship: Early Church Practices in Social, Historical, and Theological Perspective*. Grand Rapids: Baker Academic, 2014.

McKay, Adam, dir. *Don't Look Up*. 2021. Los Angeles, CA: Hyperobject Industries. https://www.netflix.com/title/81252357?trkid=258593161&s=i&vlang=en.

Meyers, Ruth A. *Missional Worship, Worshipful Mission: Gathering as God's People, Going Out in God's Name*. Grand Rapids: Eerdmans, 2014.

My Jewish Learning. "Blessings for Food and Drink: Texts, Translations and Transliterations." Blessings. https://www.myjewishlearning.com/article/blessings-for-food-drink/#:~:text=Eloheinu%20melekh%20ha'olam%20hamotzi,forth%20bread%20from%20the%20earth.

Nelson, Derek, et al., eds. *Theologians in Their Own Words*. Minneapolis: Fortress, 2013.

O'Donovan, Oliver. *On the Thirty-Nine Articles: A Conversation with Tudor Christianity*. 2nd ed. London: SCM Press, 2011.

Oliver, Juan M. C. "The Banquet of the Kingdom." *Anglican Theological Review* 104 (Feb. 2022) 22–36.

Ouspensky, Leonid, and Vladimir Lossky. *The Meaning of Icons*. Translated by G. E. H. Palmer and E. Kadloubovsky. Crestwood, NY: SVS Press, 1982.

Payton, James R. *Light from the Christian East: An Introduction to the Orthodox Tradition*. Downers Grove, IL: InterVarsity, 2007.

Pew Research Center. "About Three-in-Ten U.S. Adults Are Now Religiously Unaffiliated." Dec. 14, 2021. https://www.pewresearch.org/religion/2021/12/14/about-three-in-ten-u-s-adults-are-now-religiously-unaffiliated/.

———. "In U.S., Decline of Christianity Continues at Rapid Pace: An Update on America's Changing Religious Landscape." Oct. 17, 2019. https://www.pewforum.org/2019/10/17/in-u-s-decline-of-christianity-continues-at-rapid-pace/.

Price, Charles P., and Louis Weil. *Liturgy for Living*. Rev. ed. Harrisburg, PA: Morehouse, 2000.

Putnam, Robert D., and Lewis M. Feldstein. *Better Together: Restoring the American Community*. New York: Simon & Schuster, 2003.

Ramsey, Arthur Michael. *The Glory of God and the Transfiguration of Christ*. London: Libra, 1967.

Ramsey, Michael. *The Anglican Spirit*. Edited by Dale Coleman. New York: Church Publishing, 2004.

———. *The Gospel and the Catholic Church*. London: SPCK, 1990.

Reinhartz, Adele. John. In *The Jewish Annotated New Testament: Revised Standard Version*, edited by Amy Jill-Levine and Marc Zvi Brettlern. New York: Oxford University Press, 2011.

Rodgers, John H., Jr. *The 39 Articles of Religion: A Commentary with Introduction to Systematic Theology*. Huntington Beach, CA: Anglican House, 2015. Kindle.

Rothauge, Arlin J. *The Life Cycle in Congregations: A Process of Natural Creation and an Opportunity for New Creation*. Congregational Vitality Series. New

BIBLIOGRAPHY

York: Congregational Ministries Cluster, Episcopal Church Center, n.d., ca. 1995.

Sarna, Nahum M. *Genesis*. The JPS Torah Commentary. Philadelphia: Jewish Publication Society, 1989.

Sensing, Tim. *Qualitative Research: A Multi-methods Approach to Projects for Doctor of Ministry Theses*. Eugene, OR: Wipf & Stock, 2011.

Society of Biblical Literature (SBL). *The SBL Study Bible*. New York: HarperOne, 2023.

Soloveitchik, Joseph B. *The Lonely Man of Faith*. New York: Doubleday, 2006. Kindle.

Talley, Thomas J. *The Origins of the Liturgical Year*. Collegeville, MN: Liturgical Press, 1986.

Task Force on Liturgical Prayer and Prayer Book Revision. "Principles to Guide the Development of Liturgical Texts." Oct. 2019. https://www.episcopalcommonprayer.org/uploads/1/2/3/0/123026473/principles_for_new_liturgical_text_-_tflpbr_draft_10-24-19.pdf.

Thiselton, Anthony C. *1 Corinthians: A Shorter Exegetical and Pastoral Commentary*. Grand Rapids: Eerdmans, 2011. Kindle.

Tickle, Phyllis. *The Great Emergence: How Christianity Is Changing and Why*. Grand Rapids: Baker Books, 2012.

Verrill, Robert. "A–Z of the Mass: Berakah." Dominican Friars of the English Province, July 7, 2010. https://www.english.op.org/godzdogz/a-z-of-the-mass-berakah/.

Vezzali, Loris, and Sofia Stathi, eds. *Intergroup Contact Theory: Recent Developments and Future Directions*. Oxford: Routledge, 2017.

Walter, Barbara F. *How Civil Wars Start and How to Stop Them*. New York: Crown, 2022.

Weil, Louis. *A Theology of Worship*. Cambridge, MA: Cowley Publications, 2002.

Willett, Walter C. *Eat, Drink, and Be Healthy: The Harvard Medical School Guide to Healthy Eating*. New York: Free Press, 2017.

Name/Subject Index

Page numbers referring to figures are in *italics*.

Abraham, story of Lazarus and, 37
Abraham and Sarah
    churches as heirs of through adaptive leadership, 77
    eucharistic meal and, 55
    glory of, 15
    story of, 12–13
    transcending normal human rationality, 18
Adam, Jesus Christ as through baptism, 27, 44–46
Adam, meaning "human," 3–4
Adam the first. *See also* two adams
    Abraham and Sarah transcending their traits of, 18
    adaptive leadership and, 68
    attitude of domination of, 28–29
    authority vs. leadership in, 60–61
    characters in *Don't Look Up* (McKay) reflecting, 36
    life presenting tempting shortcuts to, 11
    longings of, 77
    traits of, 4, 9–10

Adam the second. *See also* two adams
    adaptive leadership and, 68
    attitude of stewardship of, 28, 29
    characters in *Don't Look Up* (McKay) reflecting, 36
    leadership of, 61–62
    traits of, 4, 9, 10–11
adaptive challenges, 4, 61–64, 65–68, 71, 73–77
adaptive leadership, 60–62, 63–65, 68, 73–74
agape, 43
agency, 4, 5–6, 12, 74. *See also* moral agency
Allchin, A. M., 52
Allen, Gordon, xvi
anamnesis in the Lord's Supper, 21
Anglicanism, 47, 49, 52, 75–76
Anne (York Minster nun), xiii
Aquinas, Saint, xiii
Ash Wednesday, 47
authority, 60–61, 63, 66
Avis, Paul, 49–50

Baldwin, James Mark, 72–73

Name/Subject Index

baptism
  in the Book of Common Prayer (1979), 44, 46
  death and resurrection of Jesus Christ connection to, 47–48
  early liturgy of, 45–46
  Episcopal church changes to, 48–50
  eucharistic community constituted by, 42
  as initiation, 58
  new rite of, 51
  optimal conflict embedded in liturgy of, 74
  Paul on, 42, 48
"Baptism as Complete Sacramental Initiation" (BASCI), 49–50
Barnhouse, Ruth Tiffany, xv
Bass, Dorothy, 54
Berakah prayers
  as aspect of every faithful Jew, 33
  Daniel's, 32
  importance of during social isolation, 37–38
  meal, community and Eucharist connection to, 43–44
  modern relevance of, 33–35
  praising God, 29–31
  role of in meal blessing, 29–32
  Solomon's, 32
berakoth. *See* Berakah prayers
Black, C. Clifton, 19
Book of Common Prayer (1662), 49–50
Book of Common Prayer (1979)
  baptismal rites, 44
  catechism in, 46–47, 56
  changes in sacramental practice, 52
  "Concerning the Service of the Church," 47
  Episcopal Church life shaped by for modern day, 51–52
  including liturgies for special days, 47–48
  notion of berakah and enjoyment of food and beverage in, 80
  optimal conflict embedded in, 74
  "An Outline of the Faith: Commonly called the Catechism," 46–47
Booty, John, xiv
Bouyer, Louis, 33
Bradshaw, Paul F., 19, 20
bread, traditions of, xxi
bread of affliction, 22
Brueggemann, Walter, 15

Carlson, A. J., xiv
catechism, 46–47, 56
Catholic Worker tradition, 53–54
Chalamet, Timothée, 35
change, hidden competing commitments to, 70–71
change, resisting, 62–63, 65, 69–72
Christ Jesus. *See* Jesus Christ
christomorphic Christian self, 56–57
"church," etymology of and loss of the notion of household, 39–41
Church of England, xvi, 47
churches. *See also* Episcopal Church
  Adam the first and second gifts knowledge of, 76–77

Name/Subject Index

berakah's meaning
  minimized by, 43
as the body of Christ, 17, 27
Church of England, xvi, 47
detracting from fullness of
  anamnesis in the Lord's
  Supper, 21–22
as heirs of the faith of
  Abraham and Sarah, 77
mission of, according to
  the Book of Common
  Prayer (1979), 46–47
Coakley, Sarah, xviii, 17–18
Cohen, Shaye J. D., 42
communion, 40–41, 42–43, 48, 49–50
communities, xxi–xxii, 12, 55, 62–65
compassion, 4, 18. *See also*
  Adam the second
confirmation, 49, 52
contact hypothesis, 55
Cook, Michael, 45
Corinthians (people), 21–23
covenant in Christ's blood, 22
COVID-19 pandemic, xix, 28, 33
Cox, Harvey, xviii
creation
  as God's first gift, xxi–xxii
  in Hebrew scriptures, 3
  humankind's role in, 5, 7–8
  redemption wrought on the
    ground of, 77
  role of in blessings, 29–31
  role of in the partaking of
    food, 37–38
  the two adams and, 9, 11, 28–29
  two stories of, 3, 6

Daniel, 32
Davison, Andrew, 29
Dead Sea Scrolls, 30

Denn, Wendy, xviii
Deuteronomy, book of, 5–6
disequilibrium, communities in, 62–65
Dominiak, Paul, 58–59, 75
Don't Look Up (McKay), 34–36
Drew, Mark, 43–44
Dykstra, Craig, 54

Easter, great vigil of, 47–48
Elohim, 9
Episcopal Church. *See also* Book
  of Common Prayer
  (1979)
  baptism and, 40–41, 44, 48–50
  Book of Common Prayer
    (1979) shaping for
    modern day, 51–52
  full participation of the
    baptized in, 50–52
  Standing Liturgical
    Commission of, 50
eschatological banquet, 54–55, 77
eschatological dimension of the
  Eucharist, 41, 42–43
eschatological glory, 58–59
Eucharist
  Book of Common Prayer
    (1979), 47
  as continual degrees of
    growth, 58–59
  in the early days of
    Christianity, 41
  eschatological dimension of, 41–43
  as full meal, xv
  as literal feeding of body and
    soul, 24
  meal, community and
    the Berakah prayer
    connection, 43–44

Eucharist (*continued*)
   optimal conflict embedded in, 74
   as sign and evidence of a new world, 53
   source of, 20
eucharistic meals. *See also* Lord's Supper
   as continuation of hospitality of Abraham and Sarah, 55
   early Christians and, 23
   guidance for, 78–80
   intergroup contact and, 55–56
   Isaiah's vision of, 54
   Paschal, 43–44
   reduction of minimizing the experience of God, 53
   social distinctions dissolved in, 42
Exodus Passover, 22

faith
   baptismal and following the law, 42
   in *Don't Look Up* (McKay), 35–36
   as infused "intellectual habit of the mind," 75
   loneliness created by acts of, 11–12
   in the story of Abraham and Sarah, 14–15, 18
family systems theory, 75
Ferrazzi, Keith, 55
food
   in 1 Corinthians, 22–23
   in Genesis, 7–8
   giving versus sharing, 36
   role of creation in partaking of, 37–38
   savoring during eucharistic meals, 78–80
   in the story of Sarah and Abraham, 13–14
   views of the two adams on, 36
Ford, David, xvi, 30–31
Fout, Jason, xix, 7, 56–57
Fowler, James, xv, xvi

Genesis, book of
   Abraham and Sarah story in, 12–14
   agency discussed in, 4–5
   dominion of humanity in, 5
   food discussed in, 7–8
   human place in creation in, 7–8
   two creation stories in, 3, 6
glory
   of Abraham and Sarah, 15
   baptismal reflection of, 44–46
   in human agency, 12
   humankind form of, 7–8
   lifelong transformation into the "full stature of Christ" and, 56–59, 74–75, 77
   role of in Berakah prayers, 29
   of the two adams, 4
God
   adaptive challenges/leadership and, 66–67, 68–69
   glory of, 56–57
   household of, 40–41
   human struggle to form likeness of, xxi–xxii, 6–7
   Jesus Christ unequal with, 45
   longing for humanity, 17–18
   praising, 29–38, 43–44
   rebellion against, 5, 6–7

Name/Subject Index

role of in Berakah prayers, 29, 31
temporal abduction and, 75–76
YHWH as a name for, 9
Good Friday, 47
Gospels, 18–20, 23, 30, 43
Grace in the Rearview Mirror (Luck Stanley), xi
gratitude
  Jesus Christ feeding the multitudes as act of, 20
  lack of, 36, 37
  role of in baptism, 46
  role of in blessings, 29–33, 43–44
  in the story of Lazarus and Abraham, 37

Hallisey, Charles, xvii
Hanson, Paul, xviii
Hardy, Dan, xvi–xvii, xix, 30–31, 75–76
Hebrew Bible, 4–5
Hebrew Scriptures, 3, 5, 11
Heifetz, Ron, xviii, 60, 61, 62–63, 64–65, 66, 73
hodayah, 32
Holy Saturday, 47
Holy Spirit, 15–16, 17–18, 46, 48, 74–75
Holy Week, xiv
Hooker, Richard, xiv, 56–59, 75–76
hospitality. *See also* Jesus Christ
  of Abraham and Sarah, 13–16, 18, 55
  Christian, 53–54
  of disciples to resurrected Jesus in walk to Emmaus, 24–25
  Open Door residential community and, 53–54
  radical, 26

How Civil Wars Start and How to Stop Them (Walters), 56
Hudock, Barry, 32–33
humankind. *See also* two adams
  contradiction of human nature, 6
  dominion over creation and, 5
  dual nature of, 6, 8–9
  as form of glory of God, 7–8
  role of in creation, 31
  uniqueness of, 28

icon, Trinity, 15–16
Ignatius, Saint, xv
immunity to change. *See* change, resisting
Inhelder, Barbel, 72–73
intergroup contact theory, 55
interpretation in adaptive leadership, 66, 67
intervention in adaptive leadership, 66, 67–68, 73
Isaiah, 54
ish, 3
ishah, 3
Israel, 30–31

Jesus Christ
  as Adam transformed, 44, 46, 77
  adaptive challenges/leadership and, 64, 68–69
  after resurrection, 24–26
  community meals during Biblical times and, 19–26
  disciples of, 19–21, 24–26, 33
  feeding multitudes, 19–20, 24–26

Name/Subject Index

Jesus Christ (*continued*)
    human transformation into the image of, xv
    inequality with God, 45
    loving all people central teachings of, 18–19
    meal symbology of body of, 22
John the Baptist, xxii, 24
Joseph, xxii
Judah, 42
Judaism. *See also* Berakah prayers
    Christian concept of glory contrast to that of, 56–57
    Dead Sea Scrolls, 30
    hodayah, 32
    Mishnah, 30, 31
    Orthodox, 42
    seder connection to Last Supper, 31–32, 33
    Talmud, 13, 14, 42

Kegan, Robert, 69–74
Koenig, John, 23
Kohlberg, Lawrence, xiv–xv, 72–73

Lahey, Lisa Laskow, 69–74
Last Supper. *See also* Lord's Supper
    implying previous suppers and actions of Christ, 19–20, 24
    John the Baptist's version of, 24
    modern parody of, 34–35
    modified words of the berakah used in, 43
    oldest written account of, 21
    seder connection to, 31–32, 33
Laverdiere, Eugene, 23
Laws (Hooker), 58

Lazarus, 37
leadership, adaptive. *See* adaptive leadership
leadership vs. authority, 60–61
Lee, Jeffrey, 51–52
Life Maps (Fowler), xv
liturgy, xi–xii, 45–48, 51–52, 74
loneliness, 8–12
longing, 8, 11, 15, 17–18
Lord's Supper, 20–21, 22, 53. *See also* Last Supper
Luck, George E., xi, xiii
Luck Stanley, Mary, xi

Marshall, Michael, xii
Mary, xxii
Mascall, Eric, xii–xiii
Maundy Thursday, 47, 80f
McGowan, Andrew, 19–20, 22–23, 30, 31–32
McKay, Adam, 35
meals. *See* eucharistic meals
mental complexity, increasing, 72–73, 74, 75
Merriman, Michael, xi–xii, xiii
Meyers, Ruth, 19, 53–54
mindfulness in eating and drinking practices, 78–80
Mishnah, 30, 31
moral agency, 4, 5
moral development. *See* Kohlberg, Lawrence
Moses, 32, 56–57

Nashotah House, xiii, xv
Nelson, Karen, xiv
Never Eat Alone (Ferrazzi), 55
New Testament
    Corinthians (people), 21–23
    Galatians, 42
    Gospels, 18–20, 23, 30, 43
    Jesus praying the *berakah* in, 33

Name/Subject Index

meal and banquet reference
to heaven motif in, 26
Romans, 17–18
Synoptic Gospels, 43
the Trinity and, 17–18
worship restoration along
lines of, 50–51
"nonreligious" organizations, 55

observation in adaptive
leadership, 66–67
O'Doherty, Hugh, xviii
"Old Testament Trinity"
(Rublev), 1, 15
Oliver, Juan M. C., 23, 41,
42–43, 53
Open Door residential
community, 53–54
optimal conflict, 72–74
outcasts, societal, 18–19

Palm Sunday, 47
Parks, Sharon, xvi
parousia, 24, 26
Paschal meal, 43–44
Paul
on baptismal faith and
following the law, 42
emphasis of baptism, 48
on glory in Christianity and
Judaism, 56–57
letter to church in Philippi
written by, 45
socioeconomic implications
of the eucharistic meal
and, 21–23
three persons of God earliest
reference by, 17–18
Pentecost, 15–16, 48
Peter, 25–26
Pharisees, 19
Piaget, Jean, 72–73
Price, Charles, 50

privilege, author's experience
of, xi
productive zone of
disequilibrium, 64, 65
Protestant Reformation of the
sixteenth century, 50–51
psychology research, social, 55

Ramsey, Joan, xiii, xv
Ramsey, Michael, xiii, xv, xvi,
49, 77
redemption, 9, 13, 18, 62, 77
Reinhartz, Adele, 26
Ricoeur, Paul, 57
Romans, 17–18
Rublev, Andrei, 1*f*, 15–16
Ruxin, Josh, xviii

sacrament, 44, 52, 58. *See also*
Eucharist
Sarah and Abraham. *See*
Abraham and Sarah
Sarna, Nahum, 4, 5
self-authoring mind, 71*f*, 72
self-transforming mind, 71*f*,
72, 74
service, 14–15, 26–27, 53–54
social isolation, 37–38
social stratification, 37
socialized mind, 71
Solomon, 32
Soloveitchik, Joseph, xviii, 4, 6,
8–12, 14, 28, 35–36, 46,
60–61
Standing Liturgical Commission
of the Episcopal Church,
50
Stock, Victor, xiii–xiv
Stone, Michael, xii
Summit Series, 55
Suskind, Ron, 35
Synoptic Gospels, 43
Synoptics, 21

Name/Subject Index

table fellowship, xxi–xxii, 17–20
Tally, Thomas J., xi
Talmud, 13, 14, 42
temporal abduction, 75–76
Tertullian (Quintas Septimius Florens Tertulliamus), 53
thanksgiving. *See* gratitude
tree of knowledge, 7–8
Trinity icon, 15–16
Trinity of Christian theology, 1*f*, 12–18, 36
two adams. *See also* Adam the first; Adam the second
   arising from contradiction of nature of Adam, 6
   contrasting beliefs about food of, 36
   creation and, 9, 11, 28–29
   dependence of each on the other, 12
   differences between, 9–10
   discrepancies in stories of, 9
   glories of, 4
   lacking gratitude, 36
   modern parody of, 35–36
   pursuing desire to be human, 8–9
   questions of answered through Jesus Christ, 44–45
   reconciliation of, 14

Verrill, Robert, 32

Walters, Barbara F., 56
Weil, Louis, xiv–xv, 50–51, 52
Werner, Heinz, 72–73
women, xi, xiv, xvi

YHWH, 9. *See also* God

Scripture Index

OLD TESTAMENT

Genesis

	3, 5, 6, 8, 15
1:26	3, 5
1:28–31	7n9
2:7	3
2:15–17	8n10
2:23	3
3:17–19	8n11
12	12
18	13, 15, 26
18:10	14n18
18:13	14n18
21:1–2	14n19
21:6–7	14n19

Exodus

34:30	57

Deuteronomy

6:3–5	6n5

1 Kings

8:56	32
8:57	32

Psalms

89:52	32

Isaiah

25:6–9	54n36

Daniel

2:20	32
2:23	32

RABBINIC WORKS

Tosefta Berakot

6:18	42n7

NEW TESTAMENT

Matthew

6:9	38n14
6:11	38n14
9:9–13	19
10:16	46n18
11:25	33
14	24
14:16	24n17
15	24
25:31–46	26

Scripture Index

Matthew (continued)

25:40	26n20
25:46	26n20
26:6–13	18n3
26:26	33

Mark

6	24
6:37	24n17
8	24
14:3–9	18n3

Luke

	24
5:27–32	18n3
7:36–50	18n3, 19
9	24
9:13	24n17
10:21	33
11:37–54	18n3
14:1–6	18n3
14:7–14	37
14:13–14	37n12
15:1–7	18n3
16:19–31	37
19:1–7	19
22:19	25
24:30–35	25n18

John

3:8	76
6	26
11:41–43	33
13:34	24n15
21:15–17	25

Acts

	31
3:25f	31

Romans

	17
8	18
8:14–17	17n1
8:28	77

1 Corinthians

	22, 23, 24, 26
11:17–26	41n4
11:21	22
11:21–22	21n10
11:22a	21
11:22b	21
11:23–25	22
11:24	22
11:24b	22
11:25a	22
11:25b	22
11:27–29	23
11:27–30	23
15:49	77

2 Corinthians

3:7	57
3:18	xv, 56, 77
3:18a	57

Galatians

3:25–28	42n9

Ephesians

4:13	56

Philippians

2:5–11	45n15

Colossians

3:9–10	77

www.ingramcontent.com/pod-product-compliance
Lightning Source LLC
Chambersburg PA
CBHW070930160426
43193CB00011B/1635